NO MORE Here & There

Adopting the Older Child

by ANN CARNEY

*The University of
North Carolina Press
Chapel Hill*

© 1976 The University of North Carolina Press
All rights reserved
Manufactured in the United States of America
ISBN 0-8078-1278-1
Library of Congress Catalog Card Number 76-4535
First Printing, August 1976
Second printing, March 1978
Third printing, September 1980
Fourth printing, January 1983

Library of Congress Cataloging in Publication Data

Carney, Ann, 1935–
    No more here and there: adopting the older child.
    1. Adoption—United States.
I. Title.
HV875.C35   362.7'34   76–4535
ISBN 0-8078-1278-1

CONTENTS

FOREWORD

Every child has a right to a family of his very own. For children who cannot remain with their biological relatives for one reason or another, adoption has often been the answer. Rather than continuing to focus primarily on adoptive placement of infants, many agencies have begun seeking homes for "harder-to-place" children. These special children may be school aged; may be white, black, or of mixed racial heritage; may have physical, emotional, or intellectual limitations; and may come with a brother or sister. The needs of these children challenge adoption agencies.

Until now, there has been little written material about the adoption of children beyond infancy. *No More Here and There* is a down-to-earth account of an older child growing into a family. Shortly after Jake was welcomed into her family, Mrs. Carney began jotting notes in a diary. Later realizing that these shared experiences could be of help to other parents, she developed her notes into a manuscript that we feel will be of real value to all those interested in the adoptive placement of children with special needs. Although adoption is a serious matter, Mrs. Carney writes with a delightful sense of humor and practical suggestions for everyday use. She displays warmth and sensitivity to the needs of children, using a common-sense approach to coping with their problems. Her story brims with feeling and is filled with lively vignettes. How well we come to know Jake through Mrs. Carney's eloquent labor of love. She writes with the care that comes of great concern and the knowledge that comes of deep involvement. We think you will react with joy as the bonds between Jake and his new family strengthen. It is a story worth telling, a chapter in Jake's life which is worth recording.

The Children's Home Society of North Carolina wholeheartedly endorses Mrs. Carney's book and recommends it to both the lay and professional person. We feel that this book will be of help to adoptive parents, to couples who may be thinking of adopting, to professionals working in adoption agencies, as well as to any parents who are facing the everyday problems of rearing children.

Typical of most older children who need adoption, Jake had lived in many places and with various relatives before joining the Carneys. He yearned for a permanent home and family. None of us at The Children's Home Society of North Carolina will ever forget his parting words to us as he left to go to his new home. Stretching to his full height and placing his hands on his hips, he paused at the front door to say with a broad grin, "No more here and there!"

RUTH M. MC CRACKEN
Executive Director
The Children's Home Society of North Carolina, Inc.
Greensboro, North Carolina

PREFACE

When couples approach an adoption agency, their thoughts are usually of an infant, but there are some couples who believe they have room in their homes for that special child—the older child. These are the couples for whom this book is intended. No matter how determined they are to succeed (and determination is of paramount importance in adopting an older child), they will be faced with difficult and unexpected problems. This book does not aim to provide solutions but rather to assure the prospective parents that the difficulties and the accompanying feelings have been shared by others. It focuses deliberately on the child's dilemma in order to remind those parents, frequently discouraged by a seeming unresponsiveness, that their child desperately needs their perseverance. Furthermore, it attempts to convince parents of the needless strain they impose upon themselves when they strive toward the impossible expectations of experiencing immediate love for the child and of exerting a visible influence from the outset. The book firmly adheres to the belief that the parents must look realistically at their undertaking in the effort to attain success. They cannot afford to skim the surface, much less to indulge in self-deception.

The older child is defined as a child past two years of age. Obviously, the younger the child, the more smoothly the adoption is likely to run. But no matter what the age, the child whom necessity has pried from another home or who has never known the normality of family life, is scarred in some ways. He will need to learn to adjust, to trust, and to love. His adoptive parents must also learn, and at the same time, they must provide the direction and the strength for him to move. The task for both child and parent is demanding. Happily, it is rewarding.

This volume assumes that the adoption takes place

through an approved agency. There is no question but that both the child and the parents in an older-child adoption need the guidance of an agency to support them. Such adoptions arrive with built-in complexities that demand the continued involvement of an experienced party. The year or more of home visits by the caseworker will not be thought of as intrusions but welcome opportunities to discuss frustrations, fears, and intervals of progress. The caseworker will become an individual whom the parents like, trust, and depend upon. Because some parents will know few, if any, individuals who have adopted an older child, they may benefit from the shared experiences provided by an association of adoptive parents. These organizations give the parents an opportunity to meet other parents with whom they can discuss openly their moments of success and failure—other parents who can appreciate their feelings and experiences as can no family that has raised children from birth.

Because of the dearth of material available to prospective adoptive parents, The Children's Home Society of North Carolina and a parent who has received the final papers of adoption have collaborated in the effort to describe what prospective parents may expect. The bulk of what is to follow reflects the philosophy and procedures of only this private agency, and prospective parents must be prepared for somewhat differing procedures by other agencies. The brief narratives, actual experiences of the collaborator's family, are intended to serve as illustrations of four individuals' efforts to become a family, for the story of successful adoption is not simply the history of one child but of all those persons who are affected by this undertaking.

1 Profile of a Child

The caseworker arrived at the Child Care Center just in time to hear a child's taunting voice, "Santa won't come to see you 'cause you haven't got a momma and a daddy."

Fury directing his body, the five-year-old boy struck wildly at his playmate. "He will come to see me, he will," he insisted, landing a blow that brought forth adult interference.

The clobbered child began to cry. The little fellow, hard to restrain now that he had been provoked, was tearless. A lifetime of shifting among relatives and foster families had given him a veneer of toughness, and he seldom cried. Instead, his whole being lashed out at a world that labeled him a bully. The caseworker rescued him from the sure-to-follow lecture on controlling his temper. As they left the building, he asked, "Why's it taking you so long to find me a new family? You know, I'm a very nice boy."

A peculiarity of human intelligence is its need to stereo-type, but the individual characteristics of most people or places, when viewed closely, are so pronounced that the shared traits begin to recede. So it is with the adoptable child.

As there is no average child, there is no typical adoptable child. Neither predictably belligerent nor predictably timid, he may well appear as vivacious, outgoing, and cooperative as his classmate raised in more fortunate surroundings. The insecurity of his everyday existence, however, marks him as different from his playmates and is likely to influence his outward behavior. The aggressive child will more easily become a bully or the shy child become withdrawn.

The experiences of the child while in temporary care or in parental custody obviously determine the degree of his inse-curity. If he has known abuse or neglect, his wounds will be deeper, more difficult to heal. If he has been treated with indifference, he will have developed his own brand of indifference—insurance against a world that must not suspect he cares. If he has experienced love and care, he may indulge in the daydream that a family might one day want him to belong to them. But life will have taught him what possibilities equate with daydreams, that one cannot cope with the world clothed in wishful thinking. Although the foster parents and the institution may do their best for the children temporarily in their care, they can never offer the child the security of permanence and the normality of family living. The biological parents of these children are all similar in that they share the inability to raise their children, but the causes of their inability to cope are so varied that they deny stereotype. Admittedly, some of these parents do love their children. Most, however, because of circumstances of their own making or beyond their control, cannot raise their children in a manner that would produce healthy adults, and they release the child in the hope that he might profit from a sound family life. Their love for their child may not be mature, but often it does exist. Thus, the adoptable child may have known love—but he will not have known permanence. The sense of well-being that eventually enables an individual to grow beyond himself and toward the world stems from a *combination* of love and stability.

The degree of the child's insecurity may be determined by the number of times he has been required to adjust to another environment. Each time he is called upon to leave a household, no matter how poor its climate, he has less reason to believe that he will ever find permanence. His trust in adults diminishes, for although they speak of doing what is best for him, they set impossible goals. They require that he live here and there, seemingly indifferent to the toll wrung by each door he must open and close. The child quickly becomes aware that he is the pawn on the chessboard, manipulated by the adult. Paralleling this distrust of adults is a growing dislike of himself. Constantly gnawing at him is the knowledge that no one keeps him, and so he deduces that he must be unacceptable.

[2] NO MORE Here & There

If he is fortunate, he will find peers whose clear approval gives him some sense of worth. Children have a streak of cruelty, though, and the odds are that during some periods of disagreement, his companions will hurl at him the reality of his parentless life. Regardless, the taken-for-granted homes of his peers constantly remind him of his deprivation. He will daydream about belonging to a family, about being rescued by his biological family, about awakening to a day that will be blessedly routine, about being like all of his friends.

Thus, the child who is placed for adoption comes with fantasies that must be reconciled with reality. Though armed with a thin hope, he basically doubts that these new parents will keep him. He has developed a veneer to disguise his wounds from the world—and even from himself. He cherishes his possessions, no matter how tattered, for they are the evidence of his past. Indeed, he is a scarred child.

2 Preplacement Concerns

*The photo of an impish boy named Jake was smudged with my
fingerprints. "Five years old," the caseworker had said, "the sort you
remind daily that he can't play ball in the house." Picture in hand, I
paced the floor and waited for my husband to finish packing the car, for
we and our nine-year-old daughter were leaving that afternoon to meet
Jake.*

*After months of evaluation and investigation, I could only hope
our caseworker was reasonably competent in matching adoptable
children to adoptive homes. Gone was the desire to enhance our family
life with another child. Far gone was any lofty notion of giving a home
to a child who needed us. There was only panic—genuine, full-blown
panic.*

*The trunk slammed shut. My husband was calm. My daughter
was tremendously excited. There was no turning back—but I surely
wished there were.*

Before you pack the car to bring home a long-awaited
child, you will have spent many hours getting to know, and be
known by, an agency. To this end, every agency has its own
prescribed course from which each adoptive couple must
graduate before receiving a child. At times, the course may seem
nerve-racking and painstakingly slow. However, when viewed
from the perspective of a permanent commitment, the
preplacement period is seen as a sensible process that is actually
not so complicated.

Normally, application is made and medical statements are
required before caseworker-client interviews begin. Although
references are requested with the application form, they are
seldom pursued until the caseworker anticipates that the
process will result in the placement of a child in the home. The

caseworker has no desire to embarrass clients, so if applicants have been utterly honest with the caseworker, the interviews with references will be only confirmation of the caseworker's assessment. A home visit to determine the suitability of housing will complete the caseworker's report. Next comes the letter of acceptance by the agency, followed by a waiting period that is one day interrupted by a phone call that starts, "How would you like a—?"

Discussion with you about the child selected follows, and if you feel comfortable in the choice, arrangements are made for you to meet the child. Then suddenly, you realize you have completed the preliminaries, and reality, with its expectations, hits you with a thud.

Who Might Want an Older Child?

The improved methods of birth control and the legalization of abortion have resulted in a decline in the number of available infants for adoption. Many couples find today that there simply are not enough babies, and they must look for another avenue if they wish to increase their families. Of course, there have always been families who preferred the older child, but until recent years, most couples equated *adoption* with *baby*, and many homes that could have embraced an older child never veered from the course that was tried and true.

The declining birth rate, however, has changed attitudes and has influenced many couples to examine their potential as parents of an older child. After considerable self-examination, many have discovered that they can welcome an older child into their home. They have reviewed their life-style, questioned their motives, and realized that their way of living can more easily incorporate an older child than an infant. Perhaps they are beyond their mid-thirties and, recognizing the distinct gap between the ages of an infant and the children of their friends, decide they can assimilate an older child more easily. They may be past that time in life when they still have the stamina for the baby, a creature of an incredibly dictatorial nature. A couple might wish a companion for a ten-year-old sibling—a child whose age and interests will differ so markedly from those of an adopted baby that only a remote relationship can result. Another couple may recognize that they are not enamored of an infant but simply prefer the stimulation of older children. Then there are the working mothers who either enjoy their jobs or who, for financial reasons, cannot relinquish outside employment.

The older child comes equipped with several assets lacking in the infant. His potential is rather predictable; his aptitude for academics, sports, or music is not an utter mystery. Because the agency knows the child and his needs, as well as you and your needs, it can match with a higher degree of accuracy the child to the parents than it could the baby to the parents. The infant is an undeveloped personality whose potential must be gleaned largely through information acquired from his biological parents. Not so the child. Already he has demonstrated the abilities, interests, and traits that are blending to form an individual. Less likely then is the adopting couple to emerge as the sort of parents who love their children but do not especially like them. Furthermore, the child, although he alters your general routine, will not demand that you become subservient to him, as is the case with the infant. You will not have to cancel your trip to Canada, for he will be old enough to go along.

These factors may be attacked for their practical approach to the sentiment-raising question of adopting a child who is in need of love. The novice in this business of child adoption may question the self-serving motives, but motives merely constitute the vehicle that activates some couples into approaching an agency. Indeed, if prospective parents cannot pass beyond the point of self-involvement, they are not likely to become successful adopters, but if they can grow toward their potential child (which necessitates their moving somewhat away from themselves), then they will discover the individual child, important in and of himself. It is impossible to label a couple's motives in seeking an older child as *good* or *bad*, *right* or *wrong*. Most acts, later requiring us to give of ourselves, originate in our self-centered worlds. We know we want to marry because being with him/her "makes me happy." We know we want children because being around the young "makes me happy." Only when faced with a crisis that requires our subordination of our needs to another's do we become aware that we have learned to love. We cannot shrink from these commitments, even though we enter them for something less than the best of reasons, for it is only by confronting them that we move toward maturity. So too with the adoption of the older child. We begin with thoughts of how he can enrich our lives, and we grow into the realization that we want to enrich his life.

A Word in Defense of Agencies and Caseworkers

Tradition has stereotyped the adoption caseworker as a rigid, middle-aged spinster who asks the most personal of questions, and the agency she represents is known to be an organization demanding impossibly high standards of its clients. This picture was drawn from years gone by, for admittedly there was once a day when rules were inflexible and human foibles were hardly to be tolerated. The situation has changed, however, and no longer does a client have to fear automatic rejection because of a past health problem or a divorce.

Today's agency has one aim in mind—to find a home in which the child can develop into an adult who is capable of meeting life head-on. The older child comes to the family with scars inflicted by other sources. He has been failed by adults whom he had a right to trust, and he has not the wisdom to comprehend why. He perhaps dislikes himself; he feels that if no one has wanted him, there must be something basically wrong with him.

Consequently, the family must offer love, stability, self-confidence, and commitment. In the case of an older child, the agency is aware that problems not of the adoptive family's making are going to manifest themselves, and it is important, then, that the family has demonstrated an ability to wrestle with problems. When the applicant evaluates the demands of the agency in light of the agency's duty to the child, the agency caseworker is seen as something less threatening and the task of the agency can be viewed more sympathetically.

You and Your Caseworker

When the prospective adoptive parents meet their caseworker, some degree of apprehension is bound to be present. Seldom in this life is an important step taken without some fear, and adoption is certainly an important step. Furthermore, clients are fully aware, in spite of the caseworker's efforts to conduct a comfortable, informal interview, that the caseworker is constantly weighing remarks and mannerisms in the light of a final judgment. The applicants do, however, have two advantages in this awkward first encounter: (1) the caseworker's training admits that people do not behave at their best in this emotion-packed session, and (2) the caseworker really wants to like the applicants because solid homes are difficult to find.

After this initial meeting, applicants usually begin to relax. The caseworker turns out to be a quite tolerant and warm individual who has shown, by suggesting a second interview, that the couple is not going to be rejected on first sight.

The caseworker-client interviews are the most important steps in the successful placement of the child. For the best interests of both child and applicants, honesty on the part of the applicants must be the keyword. If you are worried about how the agency will view a past or present situation, you will find great relief in open discussion from the beginning. Agencies are no longer arbitrary in their demands of near perfection and, in the case of adopting an older child, having weathered some trying periods can actually be in your favor.

The interviews aim to elicit why you want a child, what you can offer a child, and what sort of child will fit into your home. Obviously, the caseworker will look for a strong marriage, one that promises to survive the years ahead. Perfect harmony is not necessarily an indicator of a strong marriage, but a shared basic philosophy and an open channel of communication are. The caseworker will want to know if you can financially support a child. Every bit as important will be what you want in a child; prospective parents often believe that any child will be suitable, but the caseworker knows this is not true.

The older child comes to you with his personality and interests fairly well set. He is not an infant whose potential you will see gradually unfold. He cannot offer you the luxury of time to adjust to his individual qualities. Instead, a young stranger suddenly appears on the scene. Obviously, the whole family is going to move more quickly from strangeness to familiarity if there are common interests to share. Adults often initiate new friendships over a bridge table when their acquaintance is too brief to sustain an evening of conversation. Over the years, they will continue to play bridge, but they will also enjoy other activities together. Your relationship with your child will follow the same pattern. A shared interest will simply give you that first block with which to begin building.

Actually, applicants are not as reluctant to discuss interests as they are to discuss personalities. Some people are not aware that they are temperamentally unsuited to other personalities, yet how often have you said of an acquaintance, "He's fascinating, but I wouldn't want to live with him"? Well, you may have deluded yourself that this does not apply to a child, but if you look beyond your immediate desire, you will find that there are some children you are not especially fond of. Do you find the withdrawn child boring? The bossy child exasperating? The rebellious child incorrigible? If you consider the neighborhood children or your own nieces and nephews, you will find that you thoroughly enjoy some and cannot stand others. Furthermore, you will probably find that those in your list of "particularly liked" have personality traits in common. You and your caseworker want to discover what those traits are.

Adults have learned to praise those whom they like but to be less adamant in evaluating those whom they dislike. Therefore, the caseworker must usually pry harder to elicit from you information concerning the type of child who simply would not fit in. You do not want to admit, for example, that you shrink from minor disabilities; you are frankly ashamed of this limitation. However, pretense is dangerous business. If the caseworker does not discover your very human frailties, you could be given a delightful eight year old whom you absolutely could not accept because of a shriveled finger. That would be unnecessary heartbreak for all.

You want this adoption to be successful. You cannot have gone very far in the adoptive process without realizing that you have embarked on a course with built-in difficulties. One secret behind the successful adoption is the degree of honesty that applicants can achieve with themselves and with their caseworker.

The Unusual Adoption

The scarcity of white infants and the liberalized thinking of today's adults have virtually shaken the ground upon which the institution of adoption was founded. Within the past decade, the social conscience of the public has been aroused, with the result that the once unlikely candidates for adoption—the healthy older children—have, thanks to the legal unraveling of laws to release these children, found permanent homes hitherto denied them. Even more surprising is the increasing number of families anxious to adopt yesterday's unwanted child—the handicapped, the foreign-born, and the racially mixed. Paralleling this budding public acceptance of a new kind of adoption has been the agency's reassessment of adoption in the broadest terms. Thus, today's agency no longer seeks homes for only the three-month-old infant who can infatuate any Jane or John. It now considers the child who was recently an "untouchable" and considers the single parent who was also deemed an "untouchable." It seeks a home for any child who can benefit from adoption—regardless of age, race, or impairment. In recognition of the fact that such adoptions arrive with built-in complexities, it looks for parents whose strengths can meet the difficult assignments they have chosen.

Because adoption of the older child is by no means the usual practice, it may seem strange to consider him as the norm, but, for this discussion, he will become so, for he has counterparts to whom genetics or environment have dealt even stronger blows. The child of Negroid-Caucasian ancestry, the child from Korea, the child with impaired vision or a heart defect or only one leg, the child of limited academic ability, the child with recurring nightmares that indicate a troubled past—these are children who, raised in a healthy atmosphere, can become productive adults. Regardless of their handicaps, these are children who, learning their individual worth, can rise above their liabilities.

Terminology can become difficult in such discussions, as one perhaps wishes to refute the use of the word *weakness* or *liability*. However, the prospective adoptive parent does neither himself nor the child any favor if he refuses to recognize the disadvantages of being different. The child who is placed for adoption at an age past toddlerhood is different, and even more so is the older child who carries limitations of poor health or racially mixed background.

Today's agency recognizes that these children have a right to experience the advantages a normal family life can provide. It also realizes that those persons who adopt such children are not necessarily the typical middle-class couples who want infants. Rather, they are the unique individuals whose experiences have rendered them capable of overcoming obstacles. Demanding as it is to adopt an older child, even greater are the demands on those who adopt the child with limitations.

If you are interested in the adoption of a handicapped

child, you must recognize that the task of making him secure requires first of all that you can live comfortably with his problem. You cannot prepare the child to face the world with his handicap if you do not have the confidence that he is by no means disabled. When the agency tells you of a specific child, it will give you all available information on his background and his present state of physical and mental health. However, you should ask your family doctor to discuss the child's condition with the physician who gives the agency evaluation. Because your rapport with your own doctor is already established, you will be freer to ask questions about diagnosis, treatment, and prognosis, about the financial responsibilities, and about the effects his handicap will have upon your life. If the child's handicap is intellectual or emotional, you will want a similar consultation with the appropriate professionals. You must recognize that no evaluation can be taken as certainty. With proper attention and care, he may amaze you with an unsuspected potential that lay dormant through years of abuse or neglect. On the other hand, he may not. It is advisable to beware of adopting him with such optimistic notions. The child comes with no guarantee. No child ever does.

The child who is racially mixed or of a foreign background presents different considerations. You must not only have an unprejudiced philosophy, but you must base your decision to adopt on a more concrete foundation than the principles of what ought to be. Can you give him pride in the culture of his birth? Can you give him pride in both races from which he came? Often the world will treat him rudely. Can you help him view these slights as a reflection on the narrow individuals who deliver them and not on his presumed inferiority? The environment in which you raise him will influence the success of the adoption. You cannot expect others to reshape their thinking. Are you close to family members who cannot tolerate persons of a differing heritage? Are your neighbors the type of people who would prohibit their children from playing with your child? How calm can you be in the face of threatening phone calls? You cannot shield your child or yourselves from all the ugliness, and because attitudes toward differing backgrounds have proved to be an explosive issue, you should think in terms of the worst that can happen. Perhaps it will not, but if you ignore these possibilities when you adopt him, you may grow to resent your child rather than to love him.

Agencies were once inflexible in their conviction that a suitable home must offer two parents. Although agencies still prefer such homes, they have broadened their thinking in the realization that some single adults can give a child the healthy permanence that is denied him in temporary care. Here again, the prospective parent must examine his way of life. How accustomed is he to the rowdiness and downright messiness of children? Is his knowledge of them limited to a favorite niece or nephew? How precious is his time alone? Does his job so drain him that he needs a quiet hour after the workday before he can muster the energy to pour a cup of coffee? The single parent cannot raise his child in a vacuum, so his circle of friends and his family members become important. Psychologists have long acknowledged that a child requires relationships with adults of both sexes to develop a confidence in his own sexuality. The single parent must determine who can serve this purpose.

The unusual adoption can work—it just needs heaping spoonfuls of every ingredient.

Can You Accept Outside Help?

Within recent years, a visit to the psychiatrist was a hush-hush affair. Unless some family member suffered a breakdown so serious as to be undisguisable, families wrestled with their problems alone and presented an intact face to the community. Today most people realize that the complexities of human experience and behavior often demand the direction of a skilled outsider. If you want to adopt an older child, you must be aware that this child is likely to need outside help at some point in his life. In early life, he has had to wrestle with adjustments that were far from the norm. His problems will not necessarily stem from his experiences with you. Consequently, you must recognize that he may very well need some direction from an uninvolved source to resolve the conflicts that arose in the "pre-you" years. Also, the problems of adjustment may be more than you and your caseworker can handle. The need for outside help may not arise, but the possibility is strong enough that you should examine your attitudes toward psychiatric help before adopting an older child.

Are You Flexible?

Because the most important person in the adoption process is the child, the agency will look closely at your way of life. The focus will be on your capacity to adopt. The very word *adoption* implies the act of assimilating into your life the personality of another individual, and in no way does it suggest that the adopted child must do all or most of the adjusting. Certainly the agency is not going to place in your home a child who is unlikely to adjust to you; rather, it will painstakingly evaluate any adoptable child in light of your specific offerings and characteristics. However, you, as the parents, will need to be flexible if a child is to flourish in your household. You must consider, therefore, just how rule-bound you are. How important is your spotless house with its well-groomed lawn? How much value do you place on activities for couples only? Is regular scheduling a must? Should children be seen and not heard?

None of us likes to think of himself as rigid, but if we are honest, we admit that, as the years pass, we settle into familiar routines. The question is not whether you have certain patterns but whether you can alter those patterns enough to accept the disruptions that the older adopted child presents just as soon as he hits your doorstep. Before you proceed very far, you should examine your priorities. You can be certain that he is going to demand a drastic change in your household. Can you give him top priority?

Will He Hurt Your Marriage?

The older adopted child will strain temporarily even the most harmonious marriage. If you think realistically, how can you expect otherwise? Visits from even the closest of friends often grow stale if extended beyond the usual three days. The family quickly grows snappish when deprived of the comfort of established patterns and the relaxed intimacy among members. Though people speak of the physical exhaustion of lengthy trips, they usually find such vacations tiring because they have departed from familiar routines.

Months will pass before the child fits snugly into your home. Both marriage partners must forego some of their privacy, some of their time together. He will intrude on your conversations, your social life, your thoughts. His very presence will generate jealousy among other children in the home, and he may also create jealousy in the marriage if one partner's absorption in this new relationship apparently excludes the other. Like most normal children, he is likely to attempt to play one parent against the other, and if he is successful, he will bring friction to the marriage.

You must realize that a certain amount of tension is inherent in the process of adopting an older child and determine whether or not your marriage can withstand this additional strain.

Are You Committed?

The caseworker will endeavor to evaluate the degree of your commitment, for your determination to succeed is the foundation for successful adoption. Commitment is difficult to measure, yet you and your caseworker must try. You must determine whether both partners are in complete accord concerning the desire for an older child or whether one partner is merely appeasing the other. You must look realistically at the problems ahead and weigh them against the anticipated rewards. You must focus your thinking on the needs of the child and come to grips with the fact that, if you fail this scarred child, you may impair him permanently. A terrifying thought? Yes, indeed. On the other hand, if you succeed, you will have restored to strength a damaged child whose future promised little to himself or to mankind.

The Financial Aspects

Regardless of its altruistic aims, an agency must be practical in carrying out its programs. Its staff members, foster parents, and legal advisers must be paid; its facilities must be maintained. You may be expected to pay a fee for its services, and this will be explained to you early in the interviews. But there are other expenses about which you must be realistic. Your child will need clothing, food, toys, and an introductory visit to a doctor and a dentist. The dent in the pocketbook is usually larger than expected, especially if his health requires corrective treatment or his limited education indicates the need for a private school or tutor. The giving of gifts, as a welcoming gesture is not as widespread with older children as it is with babies, and well-wishers, who customarily would bring clothing to the infant, will probably bring toys to the older child. In the early months of placement, you may find that your marriage demands that more money be set aside for husband-wife entertainment than heretofore. You will need time away from home to ease the strain of the adjustment, and you should realize that the extra amount of income from another tax exemption will not cover these expenses.

Whom Do You Tell?

Adopting an older child is tricky, but if you are set on this course, you will have an overwhelming desire to tell everyone your good news in advance of bringing the child home. The best advice, however, is to *be selective*. There are hitches in the adoption of older children that do not exist with infants. You may drive a considerable distance, meet the selected child, and realize that, regardless of how conscientious both you and the caseworker have been, he is not the child for you. The chances are remote, but it is better not to have alerted the whole town and then be forced to give an explanation.

However, some individuals must be informed. Your references already know of your interest and you may feel a responsibility to inform them of your progress. If you have other children, you plainly have to prepare them for the addition to the family. How to do so will vary, but children, unaware of the complications they will soon face, can usually be counted upon to be receptive to this unknown brother or sister. Because children are natural broadcasters of news, you will probably have to impress upon them that "we have a family secret." Possibly you will tell them who else is "in on the secret" so that they can derive some pleasure from sharing the news with others who also know. Just as parents-to-be do not alert their children immediately following the rabbit test, so adoptive parents are well-advised to keep silent until officially notified that interviews are ended and the waiting period has begun. Having informed your children, you must get set for a steady flow of questions and speculations as they rightfully involve themselves in the adoptive process.

Reactions of adults can quickly counterbalance the enthusiasm of the children. An adult may say, "You're really doing something admirable," but the tone implies, "You're out of your mind." Since you may have already begun to question just how smart this undertaking is, the unspoken words can easily undermine your wilting confidence. Easier to cope with is the blunt adult who questions, "Why don't you adopt a baby?" or "Don't you realize you're asking for trouble?" These tactless people at least allow you to state your platform, and convictions have a way of growing stronger when expressed in the face of opposition.

Grandparents present a special problem. Some approve readily, some support you but with private reservations (you are not really fooled), and some openly disapprove. The on-the-fence grandparents thaw once the imagined child turns into flesh and blood. These grandparents' reservations stemmed from concern for their children and other grandchildren, and now they are relieved to be in sympathy with the addition to the family. The openly hostile grandparent, however, is similar to the parent who refuses to attend a child's wedding. Sad though his reaction may make you, you realize that he is mainly depriving himself, and you hope that, with the passing of time, he will learn to accept.

Whom you tell is a personal matter, but children and grandparents *must* be informed. When you discriminate among the relatives and close friends in whom you confide, you inflict hurt feelings on those excluded from the secret, and you invite the undermining of your intentions as you broaden the circle of those in the know. You will spend many hours explaining the child's presence if you select the quiet approach, but no one will fault you for telling only the immediate family.

Dealing with Your Feelings

For months you have daydreamed about this older child, occasionally worried about the wisdom of your course, but pleasant reveries of anticipated family experiences have deadened the anxiety. During the waiting period, you more frequently experience anxious moments. Then one day the caseworker calls, and you soon find yourself discussing someone specific. A photo shows an appealing child. His background and interests dovetail with those of your family. Then dormant worries begin to surface. Can you trust the agency's judgment? Will you like him? Will he like you? Great Scot, he's a lifelong proposition! What, pray tell, have you done?

Well, if you are traumatized by the reality, you are not unusual. He is a "whale" of a responsibility, and you have to come to terms with this reality at some point. If you have been honest with your caseworker, your strengths and weaknesses will have revealed themselves. You are on safe, if fearful, ground, but you will feel better if you express these panicky feelings—especially since your caseworker will expect you to have them. The casework process also will have revealed your fundamental commitment to this endeavor, and commitment unlocks the door to success in adoption, just as it does in marriage.

Are There No Positive Aspects?

This chapter presents an exercise in caution; it belabors intentionally the problems of adopting an older child. If such a statement can dissuade you from your course, you will be happier to decide here and now to forego any plans to increase your family, and you should not feel that you are any less caring should you renege. The road is difficult and often hard to fathom. But should you maintain, "We've a home we want to offer to a child who needs us and whom we need," do read on. For there will be nothing comparable to the feeling this child inspires when one day he lays his head against your breast in the utter assurance of your love.

3 Coming Together

The child who bounded across the field, basketball in hand, looked vaguely like the little fellow of the photo—at least in size and coloring. But the in-person Jake differed markedly from the serious boy, posed with a book in his hand. The hood, drawn tightly around his circular face, concealed his dark hair. The front teeth had been lost in a bicycle accident after the photo was taken. Though our caseworker had described him as extremely energetic, we discovered that our imaginations had latched on to the refined child on film. Clearly, we had to change our thinking.

He gave only passing notice to the caseworker's introduction to us as her friends and set about demonstrating his agility. He shinnied up a pole, turned flips, and practiced shots at the lowered basketball goal. Our daughter, Polly, an athletic dud, was clearly awed. She had expected to like him, but when he began turning cartwheels in series, she who had suffered utter humiliation at her inability to perform this feat, swelled with pride at the thought of such a brother. She could contain herself no longer. Suddenly she demanded, "Do you want to be my brother?"

You will not simply meet your older child at the agency, pack his belongings, and take him home. Because of the complexities of his adoption, the agency will insist upon a get-acquainted period, punctuated by interviews with a caseworker, before he is released to you. Your first contact with the child may be little more than a glimpse as he enjoys an ice-cream cone at a drugstore counter. Perhaps you will be introduced to him as the caseworker's friends and invite him to go to the zoo with you. For his and your own protection, you will not be introduced as possible parents. Some previously undetected problems may surface during this visitation period if he meets you as his parents-to-be, and termination of the visiting process would be unnecessarily cruel to him. The circumstances of your first meeting will not be prolonged, and because you will find that you must ease into a relationship with him, you will be appreciative of the agency's cautious approach.

When you meet your child, you will meet him on his territory with his own caseworker, not necessarily the caseworker with whom you have worked. His caseworker will have seen the agency files on you and will soon cease to be a stranger. Together you will discuss the child and arrange for a meeting. His caseworker will steer you through the visitation process, always available to answer questions, give advice, and help you handle your feelings.

Your Feelings

You will find yourself endeavoring to cope with a multitude of feelings. Your child will probably not be what you expected. If you have seen his picture, you may have formed an inaccurate image. The actual child may leave you disappointed, for you will have partly adjusted to the child in the photo. Even if you have not daydreamed of his face or personality, when you meet him, you are likely to experience a painful shock of disbelief. Months later, when you have gained perspective, you will discover that your reaction was not to the child but to your moving from fiction to fact. No matter how much your caseworker has cautioned you against expecting a surge of love when you first glimpse your child, it is only when you meet him that you will understand what you have been told.

Because of the seriousness of this endeavor, you may find yourself unable to respond to the child. Your expected apprehension, coupled with the shock of meeting, can easily numb you into a seeming callousness toward him. You may find yourself appraising him as though he were a chair you had ordered. Not as handsome as his picture—his grammar needs refining—perhaps with alterations he will blend into your household. Heartless though this attitude may seem, it is necessary in some form or other. Like that chair, he must fit into your scheme of things. The agency matches parents to child with a thorough objectivity that evaluates all factors involved. You, however, probably had approached the agency with your emotions foremost and have only gradually permitted deliberate thought to creep in. Thus, when you meet him, you may be disturbed by the sudden detachment with which you view him, but the fact that you withhold your feelings at this point is only natural. He is a threat to you, for he will surely change your way of life.

If you experience a period of overwhelming doubt (and at some time before he becomes a regular household fixture, you will), you are not unusual, nor are your feelings so shameful as to warrant hiding. You will master these doubts more quickly if you can express them, and then you can return to the total picture that includes the child and his feelings.

Changing Your Mind

During the visiting period, some couples find the adoption of an older child is not for them. The many adjustments and many demands are more than they can handle. One hopes that they and the caseworker will recognize the signs and that together they will terminate the adoptive process without hurting the child and without too severely demoralizing the couple. The prospective parents who face their limitations early in the adoption effort do a service to all concerned.

What About the Child?

The child wants a home. Desperately does he want to belong, and he is terrified of never belonging. The agency seeks to protect him by disguising the significance of your interest in him, so you meet him as a friend. It is important that he accept this posture, as long as it is necessary, for if he perceives that he is being considered, the fear of rejection will engulf him—especially if he likes you.

If the child knows that he is available for adoption, he may have developed a hound-dog scent where all married couples are concerned. He may play the game of friendship but sense that you are aiming toward a lasting relationship. In such a case, his response to you will be colored by his fears. You and the caseworker then will have to work doubly hard to get to the real child. How perceptive he is concerning the intent of your visits will depend considerably on his age. The very young will be less aware. Assuming he does not "catch on" to you, his insecurity, nevertheless, will prod him into trying to please you and showing off his skills; like all of us, he will try to make a good impression.

Once he knows you to be his adoptive parents, he may undergo the same disappointment in you that you have in him. He has daydreamed of ideal parents, and you cannot live up to those dreams. Like you, he experiences fear when faced with the actual move. He is being asked to leave his present surroundings, which at least he knows, and trust that you will be his "forever family. "

How Do You Spend Those Visits?

Since the purpose of the visits is to ease into a relationship, the activities you plan should reflect your common interests. Your caseworker will acquaint you with resources of the community, particularly those that appeal to him. You will want to enjoy mutually an activity that leads to spontaneous conversation. A trip to the zoo, the planetarium, or a sports event—these are the old dependables. They take the strain off you by offering a common ground for conversation, while allowing comfortable lapses of silence.

How you pass the time need not be completely structured, especially as you grow better acquainted. A hike in the woods, a lunch at his favorite restaurant, or a shopping expedition are all conducive to establishing rapport.

Coming Together [23]

If you have other children, you will want to include them in these visits. Unnerving though their topics of conversation may be, they will be oblivious to the strain of the occasion and, thereby, accomplish a happy-go-lucky friendship that your overtures, restrained by your apprehensions and your adulthood, cannot. The sibling may very well be the child's bridge between temporary care and your home.

How Long Does the Visiting Period Last?

The length of time that will elapse between the day you meet your child and the day you bring him home as a member of your family is another indefinite matter in the adoptive process. The only certainty about the visitation period is that the earliest meetings will take place close to where the child is now living. With his best interests in mind, you and the caseworker will determine the best course for his transition from temporary placement to a permanent life with you.

After you have visited the child only a few times, you and the caseworker may decide that you may invite your new "friend" to visit in your home, perhaps for a weekend, perhaps for a lengthier stay. Then he can become acquainted with your daily routine, your family, your friends, and your personality as you cope with the everyday world. Gradually he will begin to blend into your life. Sometimes your "friend" may make several visits to your home before he arrives for the duration. In certain circumstances the agency may decide that the child's needs are better served if he does not come to your home as a visitor before coming there as a member of the family. You may visit him several times and, when the relationship has begun to deepen, you and the caseworker may decide he should be told that you want to take him to your home as your child. When he goes with you, he will go to begin a new life. There are numerous ways in which families and agencies cooperate during the time of visitation in the effort to bring together both child and parents in the most comfortable manner possible.

How your visitation period is conducted will depend on the individuals involved, not on any set rule.

You may feel that the agency is overdoing the required number of visits—especially once you have established in your own mind that you and the child want each other. You may overlook the child's need to close the chapter of his life with a foster family. The older he is and the longer he has been with a particular family, the stronger the bonds he has formed to that life. Though all of his past will forever be a part of him, he must say his goodbyes before he can successfully move toward you.

How Do You Tell Him?

Your caseworker will suggest the appropriate time for you to tell your child that you want to adopt him. You have reached the point at which you and he enjoy being together. In a natural manner, you take his hand when crossing the street or pat him on the shoulder for a job well done. You correct him for casually darting about a busy parking lot. You are able to talk to and about him as an individual. He, in turn, looks forward to your visits and talks incessantly about the fun you have shared. He has moved toward you; now he is ready to move with you.

What to say to him is an easy hurdle. He simply needs to hear you say, "We want you to be our child forever. " He is not afraid of the word *adopt*, and you should not shy away from it. You will perhaps want to discuss exactly what is happening so that both you and he agree on the definition of the word. Most of all, do not expect the occasion to be an emotional scene; children are not schooled in occasions demanding the "hearts and flowers" response. He may seem to pass off your carefully prepared speech most casually, for children are often embarrassed by, and distrustful of, adult sentiment. Regardless of his outward reaction, you can be sure that he has heard every word and now he is waiting for you to prove what you have just said.

Taking Him Home

Immediately upon arrival, Polly directed him toward some children milling around our neighborhood. "Meet my brother Jake. We just adopted him, and he can do two cartwheels in a row!"

We watched as the group raced down the street, Jake running with the pack. From house to house they ran. Phrases floated down the street: "Polly's got a brother"; "Can do two cartwheels." Then the short legs flew up in the air, and he demonstrated his skill. Though the children were soon out of sight, their route remained identifiable by the steady phone calls from stunned neighbors.

A lengthy trip, a whirl of activity, and the constant newness exhausted him into a surprisingly easy sleep. He looked so vulnerable that first night, lying in that big bed, surrounded by his well-worn stuffed animals. How brave, I thought, to have come so far on the mere faith that we would be a family to love him. Yes, he had given us his trust—tentative though it had been, and we must reward that trust with a love as strong as ours for Polly. That he become ours was necessary. Could we go this far? I felt choked with responsibility. To him, to Polly, to ourselves.

He twitched. I thought of his antics of the past three days, and I smiled. Then I kissed him on the cheek, as parents often do their sleeping children. So much for the responsibility. I had begun to care for this little fellow who had cartwheeled himself into our lives.

The day you bring home a child will fill you with pride and trepidation—mostly trepidation. If you have not yet fully faced what you have done, you will once that child is in your territory. As the news circulates and the congratulatory messages pour in, you will warm to the glow of all the good wishes that are bestowed upon you, but also you will feel an awesome sense of responsibility to this child who is really a stranger and wonder what, pray tell, you have done. You may very well wonder why any respectable agency had faith in you—and wish it had not. The feelings will vary from couple to couple, and there is not much you can do to change those feelings. However, this is no time to try denying them.

Instead, you face the fact that you are probably full of reservations about his adoption. Once you have him on your premises, he is a reality and not that long-awaited dream that the agency took so long to bring to fruition. The qualms you had upon meeting him may be nothing compared with those you experience once you have him on home territory, and if you can recognize that your feelings are not of storybook quality, you can go the next step and acknowledge that his are not either. For as you have known your fantasies, so has he, and as you have known your disappointments over this entire business, so has he. Do not feel crushed if he seems unmoved by the pleasant room you have decorated for him—even though you know he has never before enjoyed such surroundings. Accept, instead, that, as your heart did not "leap up" on first beholding him, his appreciation for a house and its furnishings cannot soar when it accompanies an entirely new life and new people. Once you have accepted the homecoming for what it is, you are ready to turn your thoughts to the practicalities of the situation.

Obviously, neighorhood children can ease a stilted situation. By their simple delight in a new playmate who has burst upon them in a most unexpected fashion, they say "welcome home" with a naturalness that adults cannot muster. While you wrestle with the practicalities, the children give you a respite from making him feel wanted. They give you time to unpack the suitcases, put a casserole in the oven, or simply kick off your shoes. However, every couple cannot depend on neighborhood children, and actually, no couple should count on more than their own resources. So you should aim for the activity of a normal day and initiate him quickly into the ordinary routine that this family life will include.

The mother of a first child is usually impatient to leave the hospital; the mother of a second baby is inclined to stay as long as possible because she knows that the baby is going to sap her strength once he leaves the nursery. Your child is going to demand just as much attenton from you. Certainly, you have made his bed and cleaned the house before you drove to get him, but how much thought have you given to meals?

Casseroles, prepared in advance and frozen, will be a godsend to you. You do not need to face preparing a big meal on that first day, and you are well-advised to have thrown together an easy casserole in advance. In fact, menu planning for several days, geared to the quick appearance of food on the table, will reward you with moments free for him or, maybe, just for yourself. Restaurants that offer take-out foods provide another avenue to easy meal planning. His favorite foods will please him, but frankly he won't care two cents what you feed him, as long as you are careful to avoid what he detests. The atmosphere you create is going to be more effective than the food.

Because he needs to adjust to your household, avoid taking him to a restaurant on the first day. Save eating out at one you think he will especially like until later, when you are more familiar with each other. Peanut-butter-and-jelly sandwiches can be a fine menu if he likes them and if they are enjoyed in a spirit of conviviality. Never think in terms of making the evening festive by serving fancy foods on the good china in the dining room. Chances are he has never known such formality and will only be uncomfortable. So start off in the kitchen on everyday china (or paper plates) with something akin to good old American hot dogs. To salve your conscience concerning dietary needs, you can always throw in a salad and green beans.

If you have relatives in town, there will be problems with those whose curiosity makes them want to rush over to meet the newcomer. Friends may have just as much curiosity, but they will usually feel you out for instruction. You have a primary obligation to the child, however, and you must keep the adult traffic through your house to a minimum. The child has come to you, not to your entire family. Heartless though your sister may call you, you must be brutal in refusing interested adults the opportunity to immediately assess the new addition to the family. He does not need the pressure of community scrutiny, and you cannot attend to making him welcome (which is, after all, your goal) while entertaining friends and family. As you have prepared the menus in advance, you will do well to have prepared those close enough to be informed in advance that you alone will determine when the child is ready to be introduced to the community at large.

If the agency has given you a photograph or if you have taken one on your get-acquainted visits, you will give him an immediate sense of his importance by displaying it in the area of your house reserved for family pictures. No matter that his is smaller than the rest. If it is exhibited in a shiny frame among all of the relatives, he will surmise that you really intend him to be a part of your family. If you do not have a photo, you will help his sense of identification with your family by quickly scheduling an appointment with a photographer. This small gesture signifies to him that he is just as important as Grandfather and Aunt Mabel, that you are proud he is a member of your family.

You may have an urge to fill his room with toys and new clothes. Suppress it! You cannot know what toys he will bring with him or what toys he will like. The same will be true of clothes. Furthermore, for a time he will need the security of his beat-up teddy bear more than the presence of a brand-new Raggedy Ann or Andy, so avoid overshadowing his past by immediately replacing his possessions. Another consideration is his care of possessions. You will not want to invest money in items that will be abused or will have little interest. So temporize by purchasing only what he needs and a toy or two to entertain him until you know him better.

The activities of this first day in your home will depend largely on the people who inhabit it. Other children may be instrumental in filling it, but you, perhaps, will have the main responsibility. Before you bring him home, though, you will know who will be a part of these first hours and how much your child will be able to cope with. You will have adjusted your schedule around him, knowing that you can successfully pass the time tossing a football, playing card games, or cutting out paper dolls. The day probably will not go as you had planned, but with reasonable luck you will feel pretty good about it. Then daylight will fade into night. Bedtime is a sensitive time for both

Coming Together [29]

child and parents. It begins with the quiet hours following supper, the hours for family games, television, or reading. Then there is the bath, and the age of the child will determine how much a part of this ritual you can become. Next you may read him a story, hear his prayers, or simply wish him a good night's rest—again, depending on age. Physical affection may not come easily at this stage. Though it may be somewhat awkward, you probably will give him a peck on the forehead, if you sense he can accept it. Thus, you begin to establish a nightly routine.

You turn off his lights and feel rather guilty at leaving him alone in the dark with only his thoughts. He is thoroughly exhausted and so are you, but you recognize that he is frightened, that a sense of strangeness has a way of creeping into unfamiliar beds at night. There is no way to predict how quickly sleep will come or how restful his night will be. Like the mother just home from the hospital with her newborn, you simply wait to see what the night will bring.

4 The Phases of Adoption

Caseworkers anticipate that the older adopted child, because of his insecurity about your keeping him, will go through two phases before he becomes, in the truest sense, adoptable. He will show you his best side—then his worst. After you have weathered both extremes, he will merge the two into the child he really is—the child who can belong in a family.

The community marveled at his adjustment. Just a week in our home, and he already had ingratiated himself to both children and adults. Never a stranger, he visited the neighbors, borrowed toys, and behaved like an old-timer. Not once did he cry or talk about a person from the past. His father and I were pleased, but this stalwartness, we knew, concealed a frightened child. Thus, we waited until he could no longer stand the strain.

The moment arrived one afternoon when another child hurt his feelings. I never learned the details of the fight, but the girl provoked the tears he had managed to suppress for nine long days. Once released, those tears gushed into sobs–the sort that enlist the whole body.

I carried him to my bedroom, where we locked the door and rocked in privacy. I talked about how brave he was to come so far and how glad we were that he was ours.

I doubt that he heard what I said, but I suspect he needed words because they, like my arms, offered this lost little boy the safest place he could find. He must have cried for forty-five minutes. All the while, we rocked, until his weight grew heavy, and I knew exhaustion had drawn him to sleep.

What a pleasure he is. So cheerful. So willing to help. So uncomplaining and appreciative. You are amazed to find the adjustment so surprisingly easy. The caseworker says it cannot last—this is the honeymoon.

You have told the child he will be yours forever; although he likes the idea, he remains unconvinced, so he is amenable. If you look at him closely, you realize that he is too amenable. You may deduce that the agency's reports of temper tantrums must have some basis; perhaps you recognize his affection as forced. No matter, this phase of putting the right foot forward, artificial though it is, serves a purpose. It enables you to get acquainted.

Soon after the child is placed in your home, your caseworker will visit you, quickly becoming involved in the relationship you are establishing. This may be a tense visit for you because the arrival of this objective observer will make you aware of the distance you and the child must travel before you become a family. Also, you must be prepared for negative reactions from your child. Some children, aware of the power the agency has had over them, will associate this individual, or any other caseworker, with eviction from the premises.

As he begins to realize that he remains with you regardless of these visitations, he will soon adjust to them. Some children come to pay them scant attention; others, especially if they are older, are able to depend on the caseworker as a confidant, a person with whom they can discuss the problems of adjustment. If you remain honest with your caseworker, you will have no reason to be disturbed by these visits. Only your attempts to whitewash a situation can threaten the adoption. You must discuss any concerns, no matter how trivial they seem. The caseworker expects difficult periods and can assist you much more successfully at the onset of a problem than at the time of explosion.

During the honeymoon period, you will acquaint the child with your community. If he is of preschool years, you will be in no hurry to enroll him in nursery school or kindergarten. He needs this period to learn your true temperament, your habits, and the boundaries you impose. He will accompany you to the grocery store, to the library, to the houses of friends and relatives. He will accustom himself to your schedule and to the amount of companionship he can expect from this new mother during her routine of running a household and this new father during his hours away from the office. You will arrange doctor's and dentist's appointments. In short, you will embark on the course of acclimating him to your life.

Sometimes parents are inclined to overentertain the new arrival. They plan trips to the circus, to the movies, to the beach. They visit Aunt Sally, kissing cousins, and seldom-seen acquaintances who happen to have children. If their child likes football, they drive many miles to see the Redskins. Always they invite a companion for him. Their purpose is twofold: to give him a hearty welcome to his new family and to ease a tense situation. However, what they accomplish is the postponement of the family's settling into the routine of day-to-day living—a dangerous postponement, for through this flurry of activity, they envelop him with strangeness and deny him the familiarity that breeds security.

How you can fall into this trap is easy to understand. You are awkward during those first weeks. The child is sad, lonely, frightened. You rationalize that, if he has less time to think, he will make a quicker adjustment. And, if you are honest, you must acknowledge feeling somewhat suffocated by his constant presence. So what could be more human than a wish to escape? However, your problem is that you cannot escape—you can only delay.

The goal of both you and your child is to establish a comfortable relationship with each other. You cannot do this if you are constantly on the go, constantly with others. Unending though the early days may seem, they are best faced squarely from the outset. The child's orientation period should introduce him to average days with only occasional treats, a neighborhood picnic or a Sunday jaunt to the local zoo. Nothing too hectic, nothing out of the ordinary. You must resist the temptation to overamuse him. Neither you nor he can long stand the pace or the artifice.

During this calm period, parents, through overestimating the ease with which the child is adjusting, are inclined to demand too many changes of him. They forget that he must feel accepted first and, although he will comply with requests, he cannot feel that he really belongs if he is constantly asked to change. You must guard against making any remark that implies criticism. You cannot alter his table manners—restyle his hair—insist that he wear his new clothes (implied criticism of his old)—correct his grammar—work on his whining—criticize his posture—break him of picking his nose or biting his nails—halt his swearing. Not all at once. You can, however, gradually begin to chip away at some of his bad habits in a systematic way. First, you must think of all his provoking mannerisms, decide which irritate you the most, and begin to work on those one or two. Aware that the child is especially sensitive to your disapproval, you must balance your criticism with praise for improvement and for other accomplishments. By the time you and he have achieved these first goals, you are ready to work toward another. If you have given him ample time, you may realize that he has corrected many minor faults just by living in your territory. Observation has shown him that others at the table use a napkin. He wears his new clothes because they are like those of his new friends. He drops some coarse expressions because he no longer hears them or because his peers have disapproved. He will accomplish a lot on his own during the process of becoming a part of your environment.

The main problem will undoubtedly be sleep. As perfect as he is all day, he will not be able to control the troubles of the night. Once he is alone with only his thoughts, faces from the past and fears concerning his future crowd in. Perhaps he cannot fall asleep. Perhaps he is afraid to stay alone, especially in a darkened room. Perhaps he is awakened by nightmares, or wets the bed. Rare, indeed, is the child who has no difficulty falling asleep. So you aim to develop patience, understanding, and flexibility. You brace yourself to accept your own interrupted sleep, you acquiesce to his desire for a nightlight, you daily change his bedlinen with little comment. You hope each night, when you bid him pleasant dreams, that his sleep may be sound, partly so that yours may be. Then you steel yourself for the ordeal of the nightshift.

If he, who yawned and forced his eyelids to remain open at eight o'clock, is thrashing in bed at 9:30, you remind yourself that bedtime is difficult and resolve to be patient, but as the hour grows later and you have grown more tired, you may find yourself short of temper. Then, again, he may rouse you nightly between 2:00 or 3:00 A.M. with bad dreams that demand soothing before he can relax into sleep once more. Thus, you become the nighttime parent of an overgrown infant, and, like the newborn baby's mother who yearns for eight hours of uninterrupted sleep, you know exhaustion and, yes, resentment. You are not superhuman. Your system, physically and psychologically, cannot meet these demands with pleasure, resignation, or complete sympathy.

Although you cannot remove these traumas, you can establish a bedtime routine that one day should comfort him. You initiate a quiet period for games or television after supper, unless homework must prevail. For relaxation, as well as cleanliness, you inaugurate the daily bath ritual. Perhaps you read to him and hear his prayers. In any case, you are present when the lights are turned off, with a good-night kiss (necessarily restricted until you know each other better) and a pleasant smile to finish the day. Eventually—maybe months from now—he will know the calming rest that you and he so wish for him.

In this fashion, the days pass in harmony and cooperation. You are becoming comfortable with each other. You do not love him (nor does he love you), but you care about him. Everyone comments on his remarkable adjustment. Those who most vehemently questioned your wisdom in this adoption now recognize the child as a decided asset to your life. You sense, however, that he wears a façade. Youngsters simply are not this good, this restrained. You hope that you have the perception to see beyond his mask, to recognize it as screening a child so frightened of losing you that he is devoting his every effort to pleasing. A family move to another town—to a new house, a new neighborhood, new friends—usually upsets the best-adjusted child even though he carries with him familiar parents and siblings, as well as familiar furnishings. Think of the added pressure your child has known—a totally new environment, links with the past completely broken (there is no grandmother's house for him to return to), and the nagging fear that you will return him (an especially strong fear if he hated where he had been). Well, you can be sure that something will have to give.

The War Begins

When we returned from the neighborhood party, we found Polly reading to a quiet Jake. Granny was knitting, and Grandpa was watching a football game. They reported an uneventful two hours of babysitting, but they were somehow unconvincing. Then I spied two magnets that were used for pinning notes to the refrigerator now on the living room floor, and I knew that my suspicions were well-founded.

Further probing revealed that Jake, contrary to strict instructions, had been caught jumping from the roof of the car to catch a ride down on the automatically controlled garage door. The door's motion carried a noise recognizable to Granny, and she arrived just in time to grab him before his legs, curved under the door, might have been crushed.

He took her reproval well enough, but when she informed him that he would remain in the house until we returned, his temper exploded. He cried. He hit her. He yelled, "I hate you!" He threw small objects. He had a full-blown tantrum.

Jake got his first spanking that night. It was surprisingly easy to deliver. It left no guilt, no recriminations, for he had earned it.

Although you have settled into a routine (flexible, of course) and can somewhat predict each other's behavior during the honeymoon, you feel you are at something of a standstill. And you are. You are still tiptoeing around each other, ever-sensitive to the other's feelings. Because outwardly the placement has gone so smoothly, you wouldn't rock the boat if you knew how. But the child cannot live indefinitely with the status quo, and he begins to exhibit those traits your caseworker warned you of. He lies a little. He bullies a weaker child. He sasses you. No matter what you do, his behavior worsens. The reservations that you had begun to lose return with intensity, and you feel demoralized at the idea of failure. Once again you need your caseworker.

You will have been told to anticipate this disturbing behavior—that the child, after trying to please you, is going to force you to prove that you are his forever family. He is putting you to his test—a test in which he besieges you with all his defiance. He will antagonize, frustrate, and drain your patience. Whereas previously you were both under pressure from maintaining an artificially serene home, he will now push you into showing your true mettle. You will find that you divert your energy from understanding him to coming to grips with him. You begin to exert your parental authority by punishing him.

The wise parent makes every effort to avoid confrontation with the child. The goal is to learn to get along with him, not to browbeat him. A child who knows daily spankings, confinement to his room, or suspension of privileges is not a happy addition to a family. So the best course is to maneuver around his defiant behavior. The system of rewarding good behavior (otherwise known as bribing) is sometimes effective. For example, to the child who insists on straying too far in the neighborhood, you might say, "If you're within calling distance when I go shopping, I'll take you to buy that book you wanted." This method is akin to the cause and effect method—just sneakier somehow. Cause and effect (otherwise known as logical consequences) says, "I'm going shopping today. If you are within calling distance, I'll take you to buy your book. Otherwise, you'll have to wait until I go again, and I probably won't go to that store for another week. The choice is yours." With the older child, this direct approach is preferable. Of course, one day you will say, "Mrs. Jones has complained about your behavior. You now have the choice of not fighting with Ricky or staying away from him for a week." He, of course, will promptly give his favorite friend a kick in the stomach. Calmly but emphatically, you will impose the consequences of his act. One beneficial result of this approach is the internal quiet it affords you. He and you both know the score in advance. A child is surprisingly acquiescent when he has made his own choice.

Sometimes his behavior will warrant confrontation. His actions, completely unacceptable, will catch you off guard, and you will have to resort to more severe tactics. You hope he will sense deliberate firmness in your reaction. You are only human if you lose control occasionally. If he responds to your spanking or restricting him by yelling "I don't care" or "You didn't hurt me," be mature enough to recognize that his need to confront you in this fashion is a clear indication that you have reached him.

Never, never threaten to send him back to the agency—this would only confirm his fears that you are not really going to keep him. Instead, when the heat of the anger has died, let him know that you regret this terrible explosion. Reassure him by explaining that, although you have problems, you have years and years to work them out. He must hear this so often that he can believe you.

This is the most trying period that you will experience. It brings to the surface your fears and your angers. Perversely, it enables the process of becoming a family to proceed. People who never explore beyond their veneers remain acquaintances only. To move toward a genuine family relationship, artifice must be destroyed. In this situation, as the verse says, "A little child shall lead them" (or maybe it is a big one).

How long these assaults last and how intense they become is another variable, but there will come a day when you realize he has calmed down, and you will feel the relief that only a battle terminated can bring.

We were on a spring vacation when we reached our climax. The argument that ensued between Steven and Jake was so violent that I would prefer to forget it. However, neither the angry phrases nor the resulting sick feeling will ever leave Steven or me. We can only hope that they did not affect the children as much.

An aggressive, independent little fellow, he seemed determined to remain his own man, allowing us only the right to feed, clothe, and shelter him. He proudly proclaimed, "I belong only to me." His rebelliousness was out of control, and he not only threatened us but Polly as well.

However, something in that painful evening must have touched Jake. Strangely subdued on the drive home the next morning, he and Polly pretended they were parents, having baby after baby in the hospital, and, at Jake's suggestion, adopting a few along the way.

For the most part, however, Polly read or colored, and Jake rode standing behind me, his hands resting on my shoulders.

"Well, you'll be in your own bed tonight," I remarked.

"And I'm glad," he responded with a sigh.

Had we passed his test by keeping him, no matter the distress he had caused? I had no answer. I only knew that miraculously he had begun to come to us.

5 His Past

There was a television program about a nine-year-old who wanted to be adopted. Jake was not watching, but Polly was absorbed in the portrayal of the boy's experiences, which she recognized as paralleling her brother's. She was impressed by the child's unhappiness in a foster home—a situation to which she had never given much thought.

So she broached the subject, "Jake, did you live with many people before us?"

"Yeah," he answered. "Lots of people." And he enumerated.

"Well, were you happy?" she wondered.

"Sure," he said. "We were rich, man!"

The child comes to his new home with both tangible and intangible evidence of his past. As he is obviously the product of this past, all evidence must be accepted if he is to be accepted. The parent who shrinks from alcoholism, illegitimacy, mental illness, or drug addiction can never adopt wholeheartedly a child whom he fears may be "tainted." The preplacement period should have weeded out the type of background that a particular family would reject, but background is not merely a genetic matter, it also includes the child's memories, his fantasies, and his possessions.

You expect him to bring toys and clothes, but are you prepared for goldfish? A dog? A turtle? A rabbit? A horse? You may be faced with one or several of these, but probably not all. Or perhaps the child possesses an article, handmade by a relative, that he treasures. You must recognize its significance as proof that he was loved and be able to enjoy his pride in it.

The fantasies, though, are more difficult to deal with. Favorite daydreams sometimes become so vivid to all of us that, years later, unless someone can verify them, we find that we are uncertain that a conversation or an event actually occurred. To the child, whose sense of well-being originated largely in a dream world, the distortion is even greater. His actual recollections are interwoven with his fantasies, and often neither he nor you can distinguish between them. You must accept what he says, however, without questioning—no matter how preposterous the statement. As he builds a life with you, the importance he gives to the past will diminish, and the tall tales will recede.

Talking About the Past

Your caseworker will have given you the story of your child's life before he is placed with you. Information concerning the people to whom he has been exposed and the influence they have had on him will enable you to talk with him without too much questioning and help you to evaluate the reality of his comments. He must be allowed to talk about the past if he is to move into the present. Giving him this latitude is a sign that you accept him as he is. Furthermore, if he is forced to suppress his memories, he will cling to them and continue to embroider.

Everyday living demonstrates that relationships with other people create feelings, both negative and positive. If we cannot express the feelings springing from these encounters, they magnify and sometimes overwhelm us. However, if a problem with its accompanying feelings can be exposed to a more objective individual, we usually gain a perspective that enables us to resolve the problem. Even if the recipient of our information makes no comments, the verbalization of our predicament often releases us from the grasp of our emotions, which earlier had paralyzed our ability to cope. Hence, we rely on confidants—be they spouse, friend, or psychiatrist. The adopted child must also have a confidant. He must be freed from the hold of his past. If he can see that you accept his past for nothing more or less than what it was, he can begin to give it proper perspective.

However, there is a delicate balance between allowing him to talk about the past and goading him into discussion. You have no more right to pry into his personal affairs than he does into yours. Besides, constant questioning can backfire and keep alive those memories. Thus, you give him the freedom of expression. You may occasionally comment on an event or individual from his past, perhaps ask a question, but if you do initiate the conversation, be sure it concerns a pleasant memory. No reference whatsoever to his pre-you years is artificial and can be interpreted as nonacceptance.

Primarily, your aim is to avoid overreacting, especially if he tells you of painful events. You should train yourself to respond in much the same manner as you would if told he did not get a part in the school play. When you remark simply, "I know that was a disappointment," he feels better for your understanding, as well as free to tell you more if he chooses.

Certainly you think it is easier to react calmly (and thus reassuringly) to a lost role in a play than to some traumatic occurrence in his past, but suppose he says, "One day I missed school because my legs were marked from a beating." If you question him for details, you will only reinforce his memory of the event (assuming it really did occur). Nauseating as the thought may be, you will only continue to nourish the past by such heated responses as, "That horrible man!" It will not be easy, but about the best you can do is answer, "How painful that must have been for you." The child can then choose between continuing his tale or putting it aside for a happier conversation.

Conversation about the past will not arise only from the need to put it in perspective. You will reminisce about days gone by, and in his desire to be like you, he may not only reminisce but sometimes fabricate memories from the pattern of your life. In other words, he may make up the sort of memories he would have had if he had been yours from infancy. You feel confident (though you cannot be positive) that he has never taken a jet to California or lived on a cattle ranch, but you do not place him on the defensive by challenging his story. Nor do you encourage him by asking questions. You simply say, "That must have been nice"—inane though the response may be. As he collects memories from his life with you, the tall tales will be replaced by your shared experiences.

Sensitivity Training

Your caseworker cannot know everything about your child, and you will have to become attuned to earlier experiences about which you can only surmise. Perhaps one day he absolutely panics because your gas tank is nearly empty, and your assurances that you will soon reach a service station do not assuage his fears. Before you lose all patience, you will do well to question whether a previous experience might have precipitated his behavior. He may delight in swimming in a pool, and even the ocean, but be terrified of a lake. He may take in stride punishment by spanking or curtailment of privileges but grow frantic when confined to his room for an hour. You will need to get back to your caseworker for direction. Often a conversation with the caseworker will substantiate your conclusions that an attitude or reaction stemmed from previous experiences. For instance, you may learn that your child had been conditioned by prejudice, which explains his repeated conflicts with children of another race. The caseworker may be unable to illumate the situation with concrete facts, but she can bring to your problem a working acquaintance with the difficulties faced by numerous other families. Together you can map out approaches that will be likely to help your child come to terms with his unhealthy fears and attitudes.

You will also become highly aware of his sensitive areas. Aware of his fear that you will return him to the agency, you never tease about "giving him to the Indians." Although you have hundreds of slides from the early years of your other children, you curtail showing them because they make him sad that you have no slides of him. This does not mean that you hide the slides in the attic; you simply show fewer and on less frequent occasions. You can understand his reactions when he sees these pictures. You cannot allow his sensitivities to dictate your every thought and action, but you can cushion his learning to live with the past.

Answering His Questions

Genealogy enjoys considerable popularity today. Organizations such as the Daughters of the American Revolution reflect pride in one's background—pride closely akin to ancestor worship—so it is not surprising that adopted children are curious about their biological backgrounds. They have questions concerning their natural parents and relatives, both as to their identity and as to the reasons they released their children for adoption.

The agency will furnish you with information that will be helpful in raising your child, such as the knowledge of talents that are likely to surface, but you will not be given the names or places related to his past. Some older children will know their backgrounds; others will have adopted a foster family's name; some will have shifted homes so frequently that they are completely confused. If your child comes to you without knowing names and places, you will be relieved that they were kept from you, for you will not have to be the judge of what he should be told or when. If, in years to come, he becomes troubled about his unknown past and you cannot help him, you can always refer him to the agency.

In some adoptions, the child continues contact with a biological relative, though only with your approval and your knowledge before the adoption. Siblings may have been placed in different homes (although this practice is avoided if possible), and undesirable though the arrangement is, some correspondence and periodic visits are preferable to breaking all ties completely.

The child will one day ask why he was given up for adoption. Your answer is simple: because he was so loved that his biological parents wanted him to have the normal family life they could not give him. Regardless of what he asks, his basic interest lies not in specific circumstances but in the sense of worth that always-present love provides.

Handling Your Feelings

The recognition of your child's past will require much maturity of you. Not only must you accept it and be sensitive to it, but you must wrestle with your feelings, many of which must be suppressed in his presence.

The child's memory is short, and away from a previous environment, he shuts out the dissension and rejection. He remembers only the good and embellishes it with his imagination. You resent his glorified version of this earlier life, but you do not shatter him by confronting him with reality. You do not criticize anyone from his past—no matter what abuse he knew—for he has developed a certain loyalty.

He may have known someone who truly cared for him and deserves his allegiance. Though you will basically be grateful to this individual (for the child will be sounder psychologically because of this relationship), you may develop a certain jealousy. The jealousy in itself is not bad, for it shows that you care enough about him to want him to care for you, but do not try to banish this ghost through disparagement. Your child will release himself from this bond as he grows toward you, and disparagement will only sharpen his defenses and prolong the attachment.

Also, you cannot let him threaten you with the past. Every child manufactures a patron saint who gives him solace when life gets tough. Every child hurls spiteful remarks at his parents, and the adopted child comes well-equipped with ammunition—idealized parents whom he will refer to as "my real family." The expression will hurt, but the best way to remove this expression from his vocabulary and its implied train of thought is to refrain from correcting him. Just speak of his "biological relatives"—a phrase devoid of sentiment. The child will sooner or later, frequently or infrequently, taunt you with, "I can't help wondering if I wouldn't have been happier with my real mother." If you rise to the bait, either with anger or tears, you can be sure this will become a frequently employed weapon. Like many barbs of children, this must fly so high above your head that he decides to change his tactics.

Fear of the past, in regard to the child's future, often enters the thinking of adoptive parents. They are giving him love and security, bed and board, plus a legal name that guarantees him rights of inheritance and guardianship. In return, they want his love as a member of their family. Whenever they read a glowing account of an adopted child's reunion with long-lost biological parents, they feel threatened by the possibility that their child will trace his background and embrace the biological relatives as his true family. Of course, accounts of children who choose not to delve into the past do not reach print, nor do accounts of the child's reestablishing old ties and either wishing he had not or, having satisfied his curiosity, returning to his adopted family.

By your adoption of this child, you have proved that love grows, that with regular use it can embrace an ever-increasing number of people. The odds are decidedly slim that there will ever be a reunion of your child and his past, but should it occur, if you have done your job well, he will always remain your child.

6 A Few Words to Fathers

Fascinated by her babyhood, Polly frequently launches into discussions of when she first walked or talked or gave up the pacifier. Though Jake never comments, I can sense that he wishes he could relate tales of his infancy. So when Polly began one of these periodic probings of my memory, I surmised aloud that Jake must have been a handful since we know he walked at nine months.

Predictably, he withdrew from a well-worn folder the seven or eight pre-us photos that the agency had supplied. As he looked them over, he spoke of his "other mother" and his foster mother. Then he commented in his matter-of-fact way, "I never had a father before this one."

One possible criticism of this manual might be its maternal slant. Because the writer is the mother, the point of view is unavoidable. However, the bulk of the material contained here describes the shared experiences of a husband and wife. The father has by no means been merely a spectator in the adoption of Jake.

Irrespective of the beliefs of those who decry the maternal dominance in the raising of children, the fact remains that, in the typical American family, the father spends his day at work whereas the mother remains at home. Even if she works outside the home, the mother's primary obligation is to her family. Thus, the older adopted child will probably be placed with a family in which the mother arranges appointments, confers with teachers, and supervises playmates. Because she is more involved with the practical side of the child's assimilation into the family, she may appear the more important figure. Certainly, she will get to know him more quickly, but her success in accomplishing a smooth transition for the family will hinge largely upon the support she receives from her husband. The family cannot afford for the father to play a passive role.

The child needs a father—the final authority, the companion in interests, the model for the boy or the prejudiced admirer for the girl. The older child seeks normality, and today's normal family requires a masculine member who loves the child but, because of the demands of his work, retains some objectivity—the healthy sort that cautions emotionally involved mothers not to tangle in children's arguments. During work hours, his is an adult-centered environment that does not tolerate whining, disrespect, temper tantrums, or backtalk. Consequently, he is less apt to tolerate such behavior in his children than is the mother, who from necessity contrives and wheedles to run a harmonious household. The father is not drained by neighborhood spats, school problems, and the eternal wails of "There's nothing to do." Often he is not sympathetic with the mother's cajoling the child into something so distasteful as scrubbing behind the ears. In short, he puts up with less nonsense and is rewarded by immediate response.

A mother can become resentful of his authority if he overdoes the heavy-handedness or if he makes slurring remarks about her ineffectiveness. However, if he uses his authority to support her, she is extremely happy to see the father come home. She knows that her firmness is depleted by five o'clock, and she welcomes the relief of a backup man.

If you are to become the father of an older adopted child, your forcefulness will be a requirement for success. Your son may never have known a man who can serve as his model for adulthood, nor your daughter, a man whose appreciation will enable her to prize her coming womanhood. Most older adopted children have seen little of a man who offered love and security. To grow into a healthy adult, he will need your approval.

Obviously, you cannot approve of your child until you know him, nor can you freely discipline him. The years of infancy and toddlerhood do not stretch ahead. You have no time to ease into a relationship. Instead, you must muster energy and interest for late-afternoon swims, bedtime stories, and family games. When you drive to the store for a loaf of bread, you should extend him an invitation. You must remind yourself that your child cannot change from stranger to old shoe until he is certain that he counts with you. Although he will more frequently cry for a mother, he will draw inestimable strength from the presence of an approving, protective father.

If your family includes other children, you will have to put forth extra effort. You must arrange to spend time alone with each child so that you can assure the newcomer and predecessor(s) of their importance. Perhaps you will take time on Saturday for one and time on Sunday for the other. Perhaps you will play Go Fishing with the younger while the older does homework and reserve the hour after the younger's bedtime for gin rummy with the older. How you distribute the time is not important as long as you are equitable in the division. Children have an innate sense of fair play.

Supporting your wife through the period of adjustment is mandatory. With your child most of the day, she will feel more acutely the strain of incorporating him into the family. Because she becomes acquainted with his peculiarities, his fears, and his delights before you do, she has information to share that will quicken your adjustment to him. She will need to discuss problems that a friend who has never adopted an older child cannot help her with, and she will require some relief from his constant presence—a relief that only you can give her.

You will be wise to expect some changes in your wife. If previously she asked you first what happened at work, she is now likely to launch, immediately upon your homecoming, into the ingredients of her day. She will not have the patience to endure a description of your day's high and low spots before she regales you with hers. Furthermore, she is going to be tired. Because you must rest up for the coming workday, she will take the nightshift, which may leave her weary for several months.

You, therefore, must curb your jealousy of her time and energies with the recognition that, if she were not a woman who could become a fanatic over a scarred child, she would not be the wife you wanted. As the child adjusts, she will return to her familiar self, the wife as well as the mother.

You can ease this period of apparent separation from your spouse by insisting on evenings out. She may worry about leaving the child with a sitter, but once she realizes he has survived her going, she will be grateful that you have established a time for just the two of you. She needs to be a wife as much as you need her to be.

Obviously the father cannot be a bystander in the adoptive process; he must absorb as much information on the realities of adopting an older child as does the mother. He cannot be her confidant-advisor nor the child's father if he is passive. He cannot be a stabilizing influence in his home if his participation is limited only to eating and sleeping in the same quarters with his family. The family needs a father, not a boarding-house guest.

7 Sibling Rivalries

The children were playing a spirited game of Sorry, occasionally interrupted by arguments over Jake's practicing headstands between turns. I paid little attention to this routine arguing until a tearful Jake ran into the kitchen, saying, "Polly hates me! Polly hates me!" With only three weeks in our home, he had not yet outgrown his sensitivity to her disapproval.

An irritated Polly quickly followed him. "I don't hate you, Jake. I love you," she explained. "Cause God says we have to love our enemies."

Any reputable book on child raising covers the normal rivalries among siblings, and the advice concerning special privileges, extra praise, and deliberate companionship with parents applies just as aptly in the case of the adopted older child. In fact, the problem of competition may be even more intense when an older child is adopted, especially when an only child or the youngest child is accustomed to all of the family attention. You may be told by well-meaning friends that the adjustment is most difficult for Number 1 (the number used to define order of appearance in the home, not importance). Such comparisons cannot be validated, but they will serve to curb your impatience with Number 1, who now becomes jealous, babyish, and arbitrary. Your situation is something like this:

Number 1 is delighted to have a new brother or sister. Then, as you begin to devote yourself to making Number 2 feel at home, Number 1 realizes that life has changed and fears he is going to be nosed right out of the family. He may also be reacting to friends who, for awhile, are intrigued with Number 2 and consequently side with him against Number 1. Meanwhile, Number 2, in trying to make his own place, is perfectly happy to edge out Number 1—especially if Number 2 is an aggressive child. Your task, then, is to prove to both children that Number 1 will not be cast aside and, since love grows with use, there will always be enough for everyone.

You may be tempted to impress on Number 1 that Number 2 has had a hard life, unlike Number 1. This approach will not work. In the first place, Number 1 is not inclined to care about Number 2's problems when he is having problems of his own. Thus, your solicitude for the newcomer may only reinforce Number 1's doubts about his security because your pleas arise from concern for his rival rather than for him. Secondly, although your appeal may seem to go unheard, you can be certain that Number 1 has stored the content of your message to later pass on to the rival. What you have said about Number 2's background will never sound quite the same as you had intended. Even if, by some miracle, Number 1 repeats verbatim what you have said, the newcomer is unlikely to accept this playback in the spirit you had intended.

You must be careful of what you tell Number 1 about the newcomer's background. Number 1 will be curious because he does not know the people and places that inhabit the child's past. He will ask about the foster family, the institution, the "real" parents (an expression children often use), as well as why the child was offered for adoption. Both children need the freedom to talk about the newcomer's past, but you do not want Number 1 to have knowledge of any unpleasant aspects of the newcomer's past. Memories that should be dismissed are more quickly forgotten if not shared with others.

One potential problem that the child-raising books neglect is the parents' misguided efforts to make the children constant companions. Already Number 1 has his own friendships and interests and must be allowed to continue them in his old pattern. A good ground rule to insure privacy is to permit each child to refuse the other the right to enter his bedroom, and there should be no borrowing of toys without permission of the owner. If you do not force the issue, Number 1 will probably initiate invitations to the newcomer rather frequently anyway. If you do insist on constant companionship, you create more resentment in Number 1. Therefore, you encourage Number 2 to make his own way through invitations, day camps, and afternoons at the park or pool. If he is of school age, he has a ready-made avenue. Regardless, the responsibility is yours and his—not Number 1's.

You must anticipate that Number 1's behavior will reflect his insecurity in regard to this once-looked-forward-to adoption. In the competition for your attention, he may become babyish, sullen, argumentative, or, conceivably, too good to be true. He will demand every bit as much sensitivity as does his rival. If he becomes a homebody and refuses to attend that camp for which you have paid a nonreturnable deposit, you must stomach the financial loss and rejoice that you had not paid the entire fee. You cannot afford to reject him (in his mind) by pushing him out of the nest at this point. If he turns into a hypochondriac, you will have to discriminate between the real and the imagined pains. If he becomes suddenly oversensitive to criticism, you will have to temper your manner of correcting him. (Remember that this oversensitivity could just as well stem from wanting to make a good impression on the newcomer as it could from his imagined fight to keep your love.) Keep out of all arguments between the children, and punish *both* if disagreements get out of hand. Obviously, if one resorts to rock throwing, you may bear down harder on him, but the other child is rare, indeed, if he is completely guiltless. And, most of all, do not expect too much of Number 1 simply because he already knows he is loved. At this time, he is not so sure. Eventually, Number 1 will return to his usual self, the newcomer will feel that he belongs, and they will settle in for years of normal dissension.

8 The Outside World

The adopted child, ill-equipped though he is, will have to brave the outside world. He cannot remain at home with protective parents who, recognizing the harsh experiences life has dealt him, are sympathetic to his behavior, regardless of how negative it is. Isolation cannot prepare him to go into the world with his head held high; only his experiences in that world can give him the necessary self-assurance.

An infant knows family first, then grows toward relatives and neighborhood and, finally, school. The older adopted child is plunked down into most, if not all, of these from the outset of his life with you. His individual characteristics will determine his problems. Although you cannot do much about his responses to the world, you can help to make his adjustment easier on both of you.

School

His kindergarten teacher was tense with anger and, perhaps, with the uncertainty of dealing with an unknown parent. But knowing this teacher's reputation, I had no qualms about her sense of fairness. I also knew my son Jake—active, quick, rebellious—and my only surprise was that he had lasted five weeks before I was called to the school.

This was no teacher-behind-the-desk conference. Completely wrought up, she paced the floor as she listed his offenses: "He disturbs the class at naptime. He does what he wants when he wants to. He cons the other children out of their snacks. And if I don't stand over him in the cafeteria, he tells them what he wants off their trays, and they give it to him."

I accepted her every complaint and felt empathy with her frustrations in dealing with him, for he had provoked me into behavior I

had never thought possible (such as backhanding him near the
mouth with my ring finger—even the blood had given me no
feeling of remorse). Oh, I felt nothing for this teacher but
sympathy. Agreeing that firmness was called for, I gave her carte
blanche to deal with him as she saw fit.

His teacher and I ended the conference in complete
accord, both of us feeling strengthened by our cooperative
spirit. Regardless of our resolutions, his teacher was to suffer
much in the months ahead, as she and Jake's parents attempted
to mold him into the public school's image of a proper
schoolboy.

The older adopted child carries his scars into the school,
just as he does into his new home. Because the classroom
demands a particular pattern of behavior, the child will
experience considerable strain in the adjustment, and it must be
admitted that his teacher will also experience strain. Under the
best of circumstances, a child who changes schools knows
tremendous pressure. Will his classmates accept him? Will the
curriculum differ? Can he function in a traditional classroom
after years in an innovative school? Recognizing these
difficulties, parents often deliberate hard and long before
moving their young to a different community. Much more
difficult, then, will be the change for the older adopted child.

You cannot insure an easy transition for him, but you can
help. Because you anticipate his problems, you must set out on a
public-relations endeavor to win school personnel to his side.
Before he sets foot in the school building, you must request a
conference with the principal (and perhaps the guidance
counselor) to discuss proper placement. If he is a rambunctious
ten-year-old boy who is fascinated by snakes, you definitely
want to avoid his enrollment in the class of a teacher with a
weakness for well-mannered girls who wear pink. Because all
school personnel are skeptical of parents' judgment—especially
of the mother's—you will footnote all of your suggestions with
an agency citation. You will never state, "I think he needs a

teacher with a sense of humor"; you will say, "The agency suggests—." Even if you have a Ph.D. in early childhood development, you are merely a parent in the principal's office; therefore, you know nothing. If at all possible, the father should accompany the mother to school conferences, partly because of his role as breadwinner and taxpayer and partly because the mother is prone to hard-core emotionalism concerning her offspring. The schools give more credence to a husband's opinions than to a wife's. You will be wise to suggest that a caseworker might visit the principal, if the school officials so desire. An invitation will probably not be extended, but the possibility of such a visit lends authority to your statements.

One likely problem in dealing with school personnel will be their comparison of your child with other deprived children. They will understand financial, emotional, or physical deprivation, and they will readily admit to the problems of a child shifted among members of a family, but you must not permit them to equate such knowledge with the circumstances of your child's background. Your child's experiences are of a traumatic variety; to benefit from the healthy family life you promise him, he has severed all connections with his past—except for memories and a few possessions. These are of little comfort to a child who longs for a familiar voice among total strangers. Though the world will say, "How lucky he is to have you," you must remind anyone with authority over him, "How unlucky he is to have paid such a high price." You must impress upon the school the severity of the strain under which he labors. You must resist the school's only human efforts to simplify his complex problems by lumping him with other special children. The odds are decidedly against the principal's or the teacher's having dealt previously with an older adopted child.

Above all, be cooperative—no matter the cost to your pride, for you will probably be a frequent visitor to the principal's office. Your child needs for you to be welcome.

If you infer from the tone of this section that you must be on guard against the school hierarchy, you are entirely correct.

Not only will the classroom be his greatest influence outside your home, but it can become an invading force. You can diminish its threat to your shaky adjustment by exercising some forethought, for you wish to avoid school problems that will require at-home attention.

Following the meeting with the principal, you must request a conference with your child's assigned teacher, preferably before your child enters the building. Upon acknowledging the imposition of a child with special problems upon this already over-crowded classroom, you assure the teacher of cooperation in backing up any of the teacher's decisions. Then you explain the special circumstances of his adoption, his particular strengths and weaknesses—always citing the agency. In short, you enlist the teacher's aid by being candid, cooperative, and in possession of agency ammunition. If your child has been placed properly, you will find, as the year progresses, that you no longer need the authority of the agency to influence the teacher to listen to you.

Unquestionably, you must establish good rapport with the school personnel. Your child will be rare, indeed, if he has no difficult adjustment problems. In the first place, his pillar-to-post life will have rendered him less emotionally mature than his classmates. Thus, whether he be retiring or aggressive, he will go to the extreme within the classroom regimentation. Regardless of his basic intelligence, he is likely to be a year or two behind his age group in most respects. Most important, he is having to adjust to a totally new environment—home and community—so the necessarily structured demands of school present him with a potentially explosive situation. A sympathetic teacher can make both his life and yours much easier.

You must be realistic in your expectations concerning your child's scholastic ability. The agency will have informed you of what testing and time have indicated his potential to be. If he has changed schools frequently (and schools are not standardized in either their curricula or in their approach to education), his achievement will have fallen behind that of his peers. If no one has previously cared about his school work, he will have developed a casual attitude that has impeded his learning, and the trauma of earlier insecurity may well have left little room for concentration on studies.

Because you know that children from deprived backgrounds tend to score lower in testing than more fortunate children, you may reason that your child will now achieve more than he did in the past because he has steady encouragement in your home. Eventually, you will probably be right if, from the beginning of his life with you, you can accept the caliber of student he is showing himself to be. If, however, you delude yourself into thinking that the fifth grader who barely passes math will blossom into a statistician, you are more apt to push him into failure (at least he will consider himself to be such in your eyes) than to stimulate him to achieve average grades. Setting impossible goals for a child is an indirect way of stating that he does not measure up to your standards.

You must not anticipate any academic advances for at least a year, possibly longer. Instead, you must be prepared for some regression. Adjusting to his new home is straining him, and he will have little reserve strength for the demands of the classroom. Either home or school must take priority, and you must help him give preference to the home. You can accomplish this if you praise the slightest success but whisk away the poor grades with a comment like, "Well, there'll be another time, and one of these days, you'll get on the right track." You might even add, "I'll help you if you'd like." Just avoid overhelping.

A child without self-confidence is unlikely to perform well in any environment. If he has already known failure, he is unlikely to risk failure again. He will have learned that, if he does not try, he does not fail. Only through accepting him as he is can you give him the security that sends him dashing toward new horizons. Once he values himself—because you have valued him first—he will stretch forth his hands toward education.

Because the older adopted child is direly in need of individual attention, some parents have opted for private school; others employ tutors, whose assistance enables the child to remain in public school. Often the pocketbook dictates the parents' choice in handling the situation. Just remember that it is best to avoid being both teacher and parent. If you establish a working relationship with his school, the odds are strengthened in favor of his education proceeding without painful repercussions at home.

Neighbors and Family

You can expect your neighbors (and all friends beyond the neighborhood) to be generally helpful in your endeavor to adopt an older child. Even though they may not be able to see themselves going your route, they most likely will entertain the best of wishes for your success and admire you for this undertaking. Until your child has become so assimilated into the neighborhood that he becomes just one of the kids, they will tolerate behavior usually considered intolerable. Then they, like you, will lose patience and complain about him as though he had been yours forever. Neighborhood children will find him a novelty at first, but quite rapidly coming to view him as one of them, they will treat him as such. Relatives—being what they are—will be outspoken in their opinions.

Upon first meeting, most grandparents take obvious delight in their older adopted grandchildren. Of course, there are exceptions, and these exceptions can be disturbing. If you have children born to you, the grandparents may resent the adopted child. They may not wish him to share in their estates. They may be unable to accept his undesirable habits, which, they fear, will rub off on or hurt their blood grandchildren. They may interpret your attention to him as a slight to his predecessors. Certainly, they will note that you put up with behavior you would not tolerate in their beloved other grandchildren. If he is better looking, smarter, or more talented than your other children, the grandparents may even resent his having these assets. Because the grandparent-grandchild relationship is an important one, you may find yourself constantly explaining to them. Mostly, you should avoid tangling with them and simply allow time to ease him into his place as a grandchild.

If you have no other children, you will want to entice your child's peers to your house. Perhaps you will purchase playground equipment unlike any other in the neighborhood to afford him company until he begins to run with the pack. You will be sure to have games and toys intriguing to children of his age. You welcome his friends to your house, treat them with respect, and leave them to amuse themselves. In short, you give him all opportunity to make friends without intruding yourself on their company. You accept that he will be questioned about his background, for children are naturally inquisitive.

The well-honed questions of adults can be downright irritating, however, for you expect adults to respect the privacy of the adoption. They will not, however, and the closer the adults, the more personal the questions they will ask. Some will be intrigued by the adoption process. Most will inquire, "Do you know who his parents are? Where he came from?" They will ask you to verify the tidbits that your child passes on. The information that he imparts may very well be fanciful, for he is trying to impress his peers. You may be amazed at how gullible the curious adult proves to be—especially when he relates that your child has been on a safari in Africa.

Before you respond to any inquiries, you had better consider the consequences of passing on information. You must recall that parents often talk in front of children, as well as to other adults. So anything you say is likely to be repeated over and over. If you have no details to relate, you are in no dilemma. Discretion is necessary when you have information.

Adoption procedures are fairly well known these days (even though misunderstood), and you should not surprise anyone by knowing very little about your child's background. To say that he appears to have inherited mechanical ability or that he was born outside your region of the country (or state) gives people little to talk about. To be more specific enables them to speculate and speculation breeds extended conversation.

People who request details seldom mean to present a problem. They have no unstated motives; they are merely curious. Unless the adult is malicious, he will refrain from questioning your child once you explain that prying into his background keeps alive best-forgotten memories. Adult curiosity does not intend to complicate the adoption.

The Social Whirl

The young child debuts in a broadening world through visits exchanged with friends in his neighborhood, his church, and his nursery school. Instructed from birth on the graces his community demands, he moves with a confidence given by his family in their everyday pattern of living. His speech, his manners, his clothing reflect the values of his home, which will be similar to the homes he visits. When he enters first grade, he is prepared to push back his horizons. He gravitates toward clubs, athletic events, group lessons, and informal associations with classmates of differing backgrounds. His self-confidence enables him to welcome an expanding world.

The older adopted child has no such reservoir of experience to ease his introduction to the social whirl. As he often comes from a lower socioeconomic group than do his adoptive parents, he will have to combat the insecurities of functioning within an alien environment. The older he is, the more sensitive he will be to his lack of finesse. Consequently, it behooves his parents to refrain from pushing him too quickly into a variety of social activities.

Aware of his basic temperament, you will soon be able to evaluate his readiness to enter the world that is wider than home and school. If he has been an enthusiastic cub scout, he will probably let you know that he would like to find a pack in your community, and he may find a new pack satisfying. Problems arise, though, if the parents, knowing of a child's prior interest, assume that the child can immediately transfer this interest to his new environment in such a manner as to achieve continued satisfaction. The enthusiasm for scouting serves as a good illustration, for the scouting program follows an outline that is established on a national basis. The child, however, derives his satisfaction from a particular group composed of friends with whom he is comfortable and a leader who stamps the program with the uniqueness of his direction.

If the adopted child joins a new troop expecting it to duplicate his former troop, he quite likely will experience bitter disappointment, which may even lead him to give up scouting entirely. The chances that he will find his new troop satisfying are increased considerably if he waits until he has a friend in the troop who can reduce the strangeness for him. However, if your child cannot be restrained from immediately jumping into some activity, you can help him both by explaining to him that he cannot expect to find a carbon copy of his old troop and by discussing his unusual background (but not relating everything you know) with his leader.

Regardless of what activities he attempts, you must allow him to withdraw if he becomes frustrated and unhappy. Necessity demands his immediate adjustment to you and to school but not to the social whirl. Although you will not want to discourage outside interests, be careful not to force him at a time when he is beset by pressures that cannot be circumvented.

When He Must Be Told On

When the child's behavior necessitates an adult's reporting to you, you must caution yourself against appearing to be on the defensive. All parents need the cooperation of other adults in the rearing of their children. When a child is headed for trouble, you have a chance to stave off serious problems only if you know he is moving in a dangerous direction. Painful as it is to hear that Johnny threw a poorly aimed rock at Jerry, even more painful is the knowledge that Johnny's rock blinded Jerry.

With the older adopted child, you are at more of a disadvantage than with a child of your own flesh and blood. Months must pass before you can predict how he is likely to handle himself. He cannot be penned in the yard; the older the child, the farther afield he will travel. Because of adults' natural dislike of tattling, you must actually encourage their reporting. Otherwise, you cannot correct him. Out of respect to those adults, you never reveal the source of your information to your child. As he has not had time to establish a friendly relationship with these adults, he cannot be expected to accept the fact that Mrs. Brown reported his climbing on the school building only because of the danger involved. She, whom he scarcely knows, becomes an enemy. He needs to make friends, not foes, in the community.

General Characteristics of the Outside World

Most people whom your child meets will want the best for him and for you. Deprived children enlist sympathy from the most hardened adults, as is demonstrated by the large number of appeals featuring winsome children as a means of soliciting money for various organizations. These adults may not understand the complexities of your situation, but you can count on their support. In return for recognizing their interest as genuine, you will be rewarded, not only by the growth toward wholeness of your adopted child, but also by a more affectionate feeling toward the individuals who people your community.

9 Special Problems and Adjustments

Our early spring always brings March days that beckon us into the yard to start our gardening chores. Supper tends to be later, as do the children's bedtimes. On this particular afternoon, we had restricted Jake to his room as a penalty for straying too far.

When we returned to the house, we received no response to our knock on his locked door. Assuming he had fallen asleep from utter boredom, we settled down to coffee and conversation. After we had failed at periodic efforts to rouse him, a gnawing uneasiness commanded us to remove the lock. The room was Jakeless.

Immediately we began the routine of telephoning his usual haunts. With the encroachment of dusk, each report that he had not been seen added to our mounting anxiety.

Because Jake is such a logical little fellow (regardless of his out-of-bounds behavior), Steven felt certain he would not have gone to the swamp. A mother's fright, however, rebuffs all reason. I feared that the appeal of the "Swamp Queen," an old rowboat that several preteen boys were revamping, had enticed him to this dangerous area. Steven's futile walk to the swamp served at least to reduce the frantic feeling building with each call beyond the radius of his permitted roaming. So Steven hunted in the car and I on the telephone until a family friend, halfway across town, called to say that he was visiting her nineteen-year-old son.

The lost child who came home was not properly subdued. He had always wanted to visit Jim, he explained. He figured that this was his chance. No, he had not thought he would worry us. He was just tired of having to stay on this block. He knew we would be angry, so he had packed his pajamas and some bread in his knapsack with the idea of spending the night on the "Swamp Queen."

Although he was put to bed without supper (he screamed a lot

[64] NO MORE Here & There

about starving, but we knew he'd had milk and cake at the friend's), he
accomplished his purpose, I suppose. We extended his boundaries. He
had been allowed to wander freely for too many years to now meekly
accept being restricted to one block. We also reversed the lock on his
door.

The aim of this chapter is to acquaint you with a variety of
situations you may encounter in learning to live with your older
adopted child. Some are serious; some, inconsequential. By no
means does it pretend to answer all questions about every child.
It merely reflects the experiences that are common to some
adoptive parents.

The Really Tough Problems

Lying and stealing are perhaps the gravest problems en-
countered by the adoptive parent. Although one is inclined to
attribute them to the insecurity experienced in the child's
background, one has only to read the authorities on child
behavior to realize that such behavior is not atypical of children
at large. In fact, most adults can remember instances of swiping
candy, sneaking on the bus, or swearing (with scissors still in
pocket) that they had not cut up Momma's new curtains.

Considering the older adopted child's special problems,
therefore, it is quite possible that his parents will have to deal
with this undesirable behavior. Perhaps the published recom-
mendations of an authority can help solve the problem. If not,
the caseworker can assist in giving direction.

There are other patterns of behavior that can also hinder
the adoption process. The bully can create havoc among the
neighborhood children and simultaneously disrupt your
household by his constant bedeviling of a sibling or a much-
loved pet. A child whose former life was so deprived that he
cannot readily accept the normal give-and-take of affection can
undermine your confidence, as also can the child who escapes to
sleep for the solution of a problem.

These are all serious problems, and neither a caseworker nor a book by a child authority may be able to alleviate them. Certainly this book cannot. You may have to seek outside help. If you are reluctant to involve an outsider in your innermost life, you need only to consider your options: to refuse counseling and possibly bear the brunt of hurting your child or to stomach your pride and possibly rescue him from a path of self-destruction. Now, perhaps, you realize why the first chapter addressed itself partly toward asking whether you are willing to accept outside help.

Runaway

The child who runs away can usually be counted as one among many (adopted or not) who, from frustration or anger, seek some means of escape from the present. Unless you have adopted a teenager with a deep-seated problem (and this book does not deal with such complexities), your child's action differs little from the neighbor's youngster who hid on top of the school building until, having reread his comic books, he could think of nothing further to do. Boredom, hunger, loneliness, darkness, and often love drive them home. Consequently, your parental imagination is more likely to cause you trauma than is the child's escapade.

If he runs away before you have established a firm relationship, you are more prone to react in utter terror. Because he is new in the area, you fear that he will become totally lost or wander into a dangerous area. Actually, if he does not know the territory, he is very likely to climb a nearby tree or hide in an abandoned playhouse. Children are not overly adventurous—particularly if alone. Naturally, you will begin to telephone the neighbors and, if the hour has grown late, you will find that other children, usually close-mouthed, will readily share information. You will also find that adults in the community are suspicious of children who are out alone after dark. If they believe you are receptive to their tattling on him for his own good, they will not be reluctant to notify you when his behavior appears to be abnormal. The minutes may seem like hours, but you will find him, in a reasonably short time, closer to home than you had suspected.

For the most part, you treat your adopted runaway in much the same way as you would treat a runaway you had raised from birth. However, you cannot afford to handle his threats of running away with such flippancies as "Shall I pack your bag?" In his insecurity, he may interpret your remark to mean that you wish he would leave. Nor do you want to magnify the situation by arguing or pleading. Instead, you must respond calmly and reassuringly, "Well, I hope you won't run away." Perhaps this affirmation of your wanting him to remain at home will deflate the defiance that is driving him. If not, at least you will feel no guilt at having your remarks force him into carrying out his threats.

Also, you will be wise to examine closely the causes of his running away. You may discover difficulties in his adjustment that were previously undetected. Hence, you may wind up this unpleasant episode with fresh information that will ease your relationship. On the other hand, you may conclude that he left for the age-old reason that he could not have his own way. He will not be unusual if the problem is this simple. Obviously, his reason for running away should determine the type of punishment, and some punishment should follow. If you feel that he tried to escape because he could no longer endure some pressure, you may decide that his punishment will be as mild as forfeiting cartoons on television for a Saturday morning. Even though you have the deepest sympathy for him, you must not shrink from exerting some disciplinary action. If you really intend to be his parent, you must convince him that you will not countenance running away as a means of solving problems.

No parent takes casually his child's running away, especially as the minutes lengthen into hours. Because you are aware that you and your child have formed only a tentative relationship, you will experience some distress, and because the eyes of the community are focused upon you, you may infer that

Special Problems and Adjustments [67]

friends and family alike view his running away as a sign that you have failed him. In fact, they may evidence more distress than the situation merits but for reasons different than you suppose. Their reaction will stem from his newness, from their concern for his parents, and will in no way reflect the opinion that you have done poorly by this child.

You Brought Home More Than One

Agencies seldom allow siblings to be separated for adoption. Because the only constant factor in the lives of these children is often their brothers or sisters, to split the unit could very well destroy their small amount of security. If you agree to adopt such a unit, your problems—both in the concrete and in the abstract—will be compounded. On the practical level, you will wash double or triple the number of clothes and underwrite the same number of tickets for the movies. In the area of interfamily relationships, the possibilities for complication are innumerable.

The study of mathematics today makes much of cross products. Those who learned in the traditional manner would immediately multiply a problem that reads "Vanilla, chocolate, and strawberry are the ice creams. Angel food, devil's food, and pound are the cakes. How many combinations are possible?" The modern school child, however, thinking in terms of cross products, would consciously consider vanilla/angel food, vanilla/devil's food, vanilla/pound, and so on down the line. When you adopt siblings, you must understand cross products. The greater the number in your family, the greater the number of possible combinations.

Frequently, the oldest child has assumed the maternal/ paternal role. This premature responsibility, plus the increased awareness of his age, usually makes him the most deeply scarred in the unit. You think he will be grateful to relinquish these heavy burdens but he may not. Indeed, he has built his self-image upon meeting these responsibilities. He has directed the young one(s); he has protected and reprimanded. Why should he trust strangers to properly care for them? You must gain his trust so that he can revert to childhood. Do not be surprised if, when relieved of his burdens, this child, who is old beyond his years, regresses farther than the age of the youngest in the unit. The experiences that so quickly advanced him also have stolen much from him, and he will have even a greater need to make up for a lost childhood.

The oldest child generally makes the slowest adjustment; the youngest, the quickest. On the surface, the oldest is probably the least appealing. Youth alone carries a certain appeal, and the oldest, more than the others, will resist you because experience will have taught him that he cannot trust adults. He may have protected the youngest who can, because of him, more easily come to you. No one will have protected him. To adopt him completely will extract increased effort from you.

There is also the possibility that this unit of siblings will band together against the parents, but such unification is rare. If there are other children in the family, each child will usually select his favorite, and he will establish his first family bond with that sibling. Children gravitate more quickly to other children. Parents are often faced with another dilemma: they may favor one child over another. This makes for a disquieting situation, for parents want to care for each child equally. However, one cannot discount human chemistry (or whatever you choose to call that instant attraction one person can have for another) and should not feel guilty. Guilt eventually sires resentment. Instead, you must accept this natural partiality as a normal instinct. By the time you have raised your children, you will have swung back and forth in your partiality often enough to find that it balances fairly.

Although the adoption of siblings presents numerous headaches, it also carries various decided advantages. Because the children have the security of each other, the trauma of breaking their ties with the past will be lessened. They will be less lonely, less frightened; they will entertain each other; and, in their own way, they will discipline each other (for example, one child says to another, "If you keep on throwing rocks, they may not want us to stay"). In short, they will keep each other in line—of course, they can also cause mischief!

Sex

A child raised to share a bedroom with brothers and sisters, and possibly parents, is predictably better-versed in sexual activity than is the product of the average middle-class home. Not only will the child be precocious (as well as incorrectly informed) for his age group, but he will possibly instruct siblings and neighborhood children in the coarsest of language. Of course, you cannot erase his experience or his information. You can merely make the effort to influence him with a frank discussion of sex. Didacticism, shock, and moral indignation have no place in the sexual instruction of the older adopted child.

The greatest danger is in your overreaction, not in his ken. Though you are aghast at your cherubic nine-year-old's x-rated drawings, you should register your disapproval in a composed manner. By tempering your reaction, you lessen the chances of his employing the shock technique when he wants to "get to you." At some point, he most likely will inform his siblings concerning some aspect of sexual activity. You should expect, of course, that either the brother or sister will report to you and you can then handle the situation as you see fit.

Two areas of children's sexual play that you will possibly have to deal with are masturbation and the doctor game. These areas of behavior were once considered positively unacceptable but are now deemed normal. Once again, you will retain better control over the child by displaying disapproval rather than by shock followed by severe punishment. A child as insecure as the older adopted child does not need the unmistakable censure of such adjectives as *bad, immoral, nasty.*

Sex play with his friends provokes a more difficult problem, simply because of the involvement of other children and their parents. You realize that he needs the goodwill of his community, and this is likely to be withheld if he gains a reputation for luring children into under-the-blanket activity. You are also especially sensitive to his reflection on you; so, even though you realize that such incidents are normal occurrences in childhood, the first day he is reported to have pulled down his pants—or even worse, Dainty Donna's—you are likely to overreact.

The attitude of the complainant cannot determine your outward response; for, as with the school personnel, you must muster a spirit of cooperation. The child cannot afford for you to make further enemies for him by your adopting a defensive attitude. For the world, you wear an unchanging expression of appreciation for its concern, and within yourself, you examine the situation for what it is. Punishment of some sort will perhaps be warranted, largely because he has involved outsiders. If the report has embarrassed him, an honest discussion of the undesirability of his behavior, coupled with reassurance of your love, may be a sufficient deterrent.

Regression

The child you bring home is amazingly independent. He bathes and dries himself, dresses himself, ties his shoes. He can take care of himself. After a lapse of time, he lets you zip up a jacket, then tie his shoes, and before long he cannot do a thing for himself. No, you have not smothered his self-reliance; he has just regressed to becoming your baby. Your family has missed that period in his life, just as he has. Although he cannot return to infancy, he can slip far enough backward so that both you and he can enjoy some of the close bonds shared by parent and child in the early years.

All children regress at times. Ask any parent whose infant has edged another child from the position of baby of the family, or whose child is experiencing emotional strain resulting from the death of a pet or the pain of social disappointment. Even as self-sufficient adults, we take comfort in visits to the childhood home that gave us warmth and protection. Our place in that home gave us strength. We trust it. When we return, to be pampered by our favorite meal and by sleeping late, we allow ourselves the pleasure of being the child again. Unless we take advantage of this luxury, we are merely demonstrating our recognition of the nourishment we received there. The older child, in his regression, is paying you a similar compliment. Because he is starting to trust you, he is inviting you to be the parents who give him his sense of well-being. In his relationship with you, his regression indicates progress, and so you can relax with his regression. He will outgrow it—with a nudge or two.

Shadows from the Past

Ideally, a child is placed in a home that is located far enough away from his birthplace so that there will be no problems of encountering an acquaintance from the past. The permanent severing of the child's ties with the past is known to be a primary step in his becoming a truly adopted child. The closer he is to his birthplace, the more likely he is to meet an individual from his former life. Though such a meeting should present no legal problems, it could disrupt the harmony of the adoptive home. Neither you nor the child needs such shadows from the past.

Present-day transportation, however, has persuaded people that distance is no longer a barrier to pleasure or work. Thus, it becomes necessary upon occasion for the agency to weigh the improbable possibility of the child's meeting a person from the past against the benefits offered by a particular home. If a family seems especially suited to the needs of a child, the agency may conclude that the advantages of the home will outweigh the risks of the child's meeting someone from the past. If this is the case, you will have been forewarned.

Because a responsible agency would not think of placing a child in the rural community of his birth, you need have no worry about meeting Farmer Brown who will immediately recognize the Jones boy. Instead, the agency may know that a biological relative has been transferred to a community within fifty miles of your home. Although that relative may not be identified, you will be told to keep the child from that vicinity for a specified length of time. You will not have had your child in your home for very long before you will understand the necessity of this restriction. It will soon be evident that, painful though his severing of all ties may be, the genuine adoption will more easily be effected once the child cuts all cords with the past. So you must forego the biannual sales at your favorite department store. What are those bargains compared with the peace within your home?

The Significance of Names

Prospective adoptive parents worry needlessly over names to be used in the family. The child finds this a relatively simple adjustment. Life has taught him the normality of children's sharing the last name of two adults who are called Momma and Daddy. Since his aim is to belong to a family, he is not likely to resist changing his name nor changing what he calls you. If he has previously taken the name of a foster family (in full awareness that this is not his legal name), he has already shown that identity is his most pressing concern. He may arrive slowly at calling you "Mom" and "Dad." Perhaps he will refer to "my mother" but, in face-to-face conversations, call you nothing. Then one day, probably when you least expect it, he will blurt out, "Mom—" and your day will be happier for it. You hope that his first name will be neither repugnant to you nor the same as that of an uncle you detest. If so (and if you sense his unwillingness to give up that name), perhaps your best course is to hide behind an acceptable nickname until he adjusts to a change or until you can adjust to calling your son "Fredonia."

Special Problems and Adjustments [73]

Today's agency deliberately places a child in a home that is religiously attuned to his background. Consequently, Christians are not adopted by Jews, and Roman Catholics generally remain within the church of their biological parents. However, the Protestant approach varies from the silent Quaker to the ritualistic Lutheran, and religious affiliation does not necessarily denote religious devotion. Hence, a Methodist child may be more or less devout than his Methodist adoptive parents.

You cannot rush your child into you own spiritual life. You must be prepared to ease him gradually into your family approach to religion. He may learn quickly enough to sit quietly through blessings or to memorize bedtime prayers, but you may very well find yourself having to change your practices in an effort to meet him halfway.

His religious training may have been neglected; he may have seldom visited Sunday School, much less endured an entire church service. If not, he cannot be expected to sit serenely through hymns, prayers, and sermons. He may have to be the oldest child in the nursery—sort of a teacher's helper—until he can be eased into giving sixty minutes to worship. You may wish to initiate a schedule of increasing five-minute spans and allow him to leave the service at a prearranged time. Once you decide he has advanced to the point of sitting through the sermon, you may have to appropriate time for playing a quiet game of tic-tac-toe—insurance against his twitching and persistent questioning of "How much longer?"

If you desire that he embrace your spiritual beliefs, you cannot push him into the church. You may only succeed in alienating him from both you and your faith if you fail to make allowances for his earlier training and his temperament.

Language

The use of language can unmask an individual's carefully con-

structed outward appearance in a flash. The social climber
may easily imitate the acceptable clothing, housing, and means
of transportation of the stratum to which he aspires, but he
cannot as easily change the pattern of his speech.

As the older adopted child usually moves from a lower to
a higher socioeconomic level, his language will probably irritate
his adoptive family. But you will not be able to change his
patterns of speech very quickly. *Ain't, he don't,* and *not never*
have been present for many years, as has his regional pronun-
ciation of *tomato, creek,* and *pecan.* The influence of his new
environment will eventually make a dent, but, until then, you
might as well live with these peculiarities, for they will not create
any lifelong problems.

His language is also likely to be coarse, and correcting it
may prove to be the area of his behavior on which you wish to
work during the honeymoon period. You must convince him
that particular expressions are not used in your home. As with
his imparting of sexual knowledge, you will have to be
shockproof, though firm, if you expect to influence him. If he
renders a hearty "shit," you should remind him that "shoot" is
a more appropriate word. You are careful also to tone down your
own vocabulary in the realization that, having used these words
before, he's not going to clean up his speech if you don't clean
up yours.

The Encroachment of the Media

The story line of a popular soap opera follows the plight of
a woman lawyer who has just discovered that the infant she
buried twelve years ago was not hers at all. Because she was
unmarried, her family had arranged with the attending
physician to switch her healthy baby and one that had died. Her
child is now growing up as the son of unsuspecting parents.
After much soul-searching, the lawyer decides to search for
her child, only to assure herself that he is well cared for.
Predictably, she vows that she will never make herself known

either to him or to his family. Certainly, she will not intrude on their lives.

Now anyone who follows soap operas is perfectly aware that the matter will never rest with only her tracing the child. Once he is located, she will find some condition that requires her interference, and probably a court battle for his custody will follow. Meanwhile, during the weeks of searching, she will state repeatedly, "I must find out how he is. I worry about him constantly. After all, I am his real mother."

If you think that by not watching soap operas your family can avoid the internal discomfort that such episodes bring, you are wrong. The reunion of a long-lost biological family is meaty stuff, and all of the media are capitalizing on it. Magazines carry personal accounts that end in happily-ever-after meetings with a brother who was separated from his siblings in infancy—so do the tabloid press and the prime-time television programs. In today's media-oriented life, you really cannot escape the subject.

Furthermore, there is really not much you can do about it. You cannot preview all television programs to determine their approach to adoption, nor can you prevent your child's reading articles entitled "My Mother Found Me after Twenty Years." Probably you yourself turn quickly to such dramatic accounts. How can your child's curiosity be less?

You can, of course, try to exercise some control over television viewing. You may have some difficulty in persuading the child that he prefers to watch a documentary on inflation in England rather than this week's episode of his favorite medical show, but when forewarned by newspaper listings, you can frequently plan a suitable alternative.

Mostly, however, you should recognize that the media will present you with a certain amount of discomfort and that you must try to live with it. One way of coping with the situation is to discuss the content of the show with your child if you sense he is capable of understanding. You will not want to probe or overemphasize, but you can diminish some of his inclination to equate his situation with the one described by this effort. Through objective conversation, you can lead him to the conclusion that he is not the child of the television show.

Adoption-Day Parties

Because the memory of bringing him home is precious to them, some parents celebrate the anniversary of the child's arrival with the same fanfare they give to his birthday. They celebrate the occasion with invited guests and refreshments in the belief that they are showing him how happy they are that he is theirs. To their dismay, he exhibits peculiar behavior; he cries, throws a tantrum, or withdraws. He is incorrigible. In typical parental fashion, they dismiss this unreasonable behavior as a case of overexcitement. What other explanation could there be?

The parents, of course, are viewing this adoption-day celebration through their own eyes. To them, the anniversary is more important than the date of his birth, an occasion that they could not share. For them, his birthday is the day he began his life with them.

But how might the child view this celebration? For one thing, it certainly marks him as different. He, who so earnestly wanted to belong to a regular family as all of his friends do, is singled out on an annual basis for those very circumstances that he has wanted to escape. A child's security stems partly from being like everyone else. If you have any doubt about this, just suggest to your daughter that she wear a blouse when the current fad is T-shirts, or that she miss a popular movie because of its violence. Her primary argument will be either "Nobody else does" or "Everybody else is going."

Also, the day can provoke very painful memories for him. When he recalls his arrival in your home, he may also recall the loss of his past and the people who no longer exist for him. That day included fear, separation, and sadness. Too much emphasis on that day could trigger remembrances that need to be permanently shelved.

Special Problems and Adjustments [77]

The parents themselves must decide how much attention should be paid to this anniversary. The child's age and temperament can guide them. Just allow reason to influence your parental emotions. Adoption day was a highly personal family experience, and it should be remembered in a quiet and intimate manner.

Effects on the Marriage

New adoptive parents have the need to go out alone more than ever during the adjustment period. The demands of the new child will deplete much of their energy. Even the couple accustomed to managing several children in the home will find themselves strained by the process of incorporating the newcomer into the household. His blending into the family routine takes time. He will interrupt the after-work or late-evening hour you previously apportioned to yourselves alone. His bedtime problems will disrupt your routine of retiring together at a set hour. The novelty of his presence will occupy much of your thoughts and conversation. If temperament causes one parent to be more receptive to him than the other, he can precipitate resentment between his parents. For all of these reasons, you must resolve to periodically get yourselves out of the house.

Cocktail parties, bridge games, and meetings do not answer your needs, for they throw you with other people, whose very presence interferes with the reestablishment of your rapport. You need, instead, the quiet of the woods in autumn or of an off-the-beaten-path restaurant, a place for lingering conversation, a place that reminds you of your importance to each other. Such moments of escape are not luxuries. They enhance the marriage whose strength allowed you to adopt this child. He does not purposely intrude on your marriage. You purposely must not allow him to undermine it.

Baby-Sitters

Now that you have scheduled an evening out, you will need a baby-sitter. Your best bet is an adult (mature but not decrepit). Because you have been well-steeped in the insecurities of your child, you may have some reservations about leaving him, but you know, of course, that only experience will teach him that you will keep your promise to return. Leaving him in the charge of an adult will give you more assurance that he will be cared for as you wish.

The adult baby-sitter will understand the complexities of this period of adjustment. Better able to cope with any sibling rivalries than a younger sitter, she will recognize the importance of remaining impartial in their disputes. Less likely to spend hours on the telephone, she is more likely to read them bedtime stories, and because she will not leave the house a wreck nor assault the refrigerator, you will return to an orderly house in which the children are probably asleep. You can then proceed to bed with a calm and refreshed outlook.

Now children often prefer teenagers as sitters, and you will frequently need to use them, but it is wise to experiment with short shifts until you can determine who handles your situation best. Your old stand-bys may not be able to cope with the peculiarities of the newcomer, who may be more inclined to try all his tricks on youth than on the seasoned veteran. Also with the teenager, the odds decrease that you will be able to extend the harmony of your evening out once you return home. Games strewn over the living room, dishes piled in the sink, snacks for the week depleted and—horror of horrors—the children watching television long after their bedtime! This type of homecoming can quickly destroy any intimacy that was restored by the hours away.

10 A Family, At Last!

Months have passed and you have grown accustomed to your child. You automatically purchase orange juice because he hates grapefruit juice. You by-pass shirts with turtle necks because they irritate him. You leave Friday nights free for his little league baseball game. No longer is he the stranger of whom you are always conscious; he is just a part of your life.

Love Creeps In

Jake had been out of school a month. Regardless of the accommodations of the school and the cooperation of his parents, he had persevered in exerting his will on both classmates and teachers. Conferences involving school, agency, and home had resulted in the decision to withdraw him from school. Perhaps, we reasoned, he needed more time at home as a preschooler before he could be expected to cope with classroom restraints.

So I mothered him. He did not improve. He fought and defied all obstacles to his wishes. He also took up lying. My confidence was sagging the day I learned that he had been excluded deliberately from a birthday party and that he had crashed it anyway. It was nil after a complaint from a close friend about his lying and stealing.

By nine o'clock the next morning, I was phoning our caseworker to request an emergency appointment with the agency psychologist. Jake clearly needed more help than we could give him. The caseworker promised to call back to confirm the appointment. I felt better, sure that help was forthcoming.

Imagine my dismay when she reported, "He's booked solid for several weeks. He's already overworked, so the agency can't pressure him. He suggests you try this psychologist closer to you. His name is—"

I exploded, "You mean he won't see us even though we're willing to drive all that distance whenever he says!"

"I'm sorry, Mrs. Carney."

I don't recall the progression of that conversation. I was furious. The agency had given us this child, and now, after months of not demanding any special attention, when we were crying for help, they would only suggest an unknown psychologist. They reasoned, it seems, that we now knew Jake better than anyone else.

Angry, frustrated, frightened, betrayed, I bombarded the caseworker with every bitter feeling. "And you tell the agency exactly what I think of them," I directed. "Furthermore, you tell them that I'll never give them another red cent!"

My fury diminishes rather quickly once it is expressed, and I soon began to wonder how I was going to explain our alienation from the agency to Steven. Suddenly, weary as I was from trying to devise a way to help our son, I realized that I was fighting as fiercely for him as I would for Polly.

Well, damn, I thought, I must really love the little fellow.

He is not the fat baby in the grocery cart who entices you into a smile even though you've been scowling over the price of meat. Instead, he is the brat who rams you with an empty cart, or the snaggle-toothed girl whose whining never wanes until she is given a nickel for the bubble gum machine, or the ten-year-old who steals your precious time while he and the cashier struggle to decipher a mother's scribbled list.

He is a child. Sometimes a pleasure, often an irritant. He has already traveled some distance from "start," and because of this he can never be completely dependent. He entered the world before he met you. People whom you will never know have left their marks upon him. He cannot, therefore, ever be the infant whose life revolves totally around needs satisfied by you as parents.

When you met, you were strangers. You approached a child with a definite personality, and he had habits and mannerisms that you disliked. His potential was a mystery, and your responsibilities to him were never crowded out by false illusions. But you rather liked him, and he rather liked you. So you came home, enjoyed a honeymoon, wrestled through the testing period, and you have finally settled down to adjusting to each other. You have adjusted—and adjusted—until he has now become as commonplace as cereal for breakfast.

Somewhere along the line, you have stopped worrying about your obligation to love him. Helping with his homework, washing his clothes, smoothing his difficult paths—these everyday problems have absorbed you. And then, one glorious day, you realize that you love him.

How love enters your family, no one can really say. Perhaps you sense that your friends are bored with your constant chatter about your child's antics, or you feel a surge of pride when overhearing him tell a playmate, "My father says—." Or you refer to him as "my child" without explanation of his adoption, or you wish he had been your baby, or you wish that you could adopt more children. Perhaps you are sensitive to his relaxing his head against your breast when, only recently, he had sat so stiffly. Then again, you may not recognize the symptoms until suddenly, in a crisis, you find yourself fighting as ferociously as the proverbial lioness for her cubs.

Weaning from the Agency

Jake played in the hall while his father and I discussed his evaluation by our local Mental Health Center. Armed with test scores, reports from school and agency, as well as with summaries of interviews with parent and child, the caseworker and child psychiatrist had scheduled this conference to determine how we might help him.

In the six weeks' interval since our first appointment, Jake had returned to kindergarten on a part-time basis. Yes, he was happy to go back, we reported. And yes, he was doing pretty well.

Was he doing better at home? Again, yes, we could respond. Somehow after that neighborhood furor, which had provoked us into going to the Mental Health Center, he had swung upward. We could not ascribe this change to any specific event, but when we had told him we planned to see some people who could help us with our problems, he had begun to relax.

"Perhaps this showed him you really cared," suggested the doctor. "Perhaps," we agreed.

No one could state absolutely what had precipitated his about face. He simply had relaxed—overnight, it seemed—as though all of his antics had exhausted him.

"Frankly," said the doctor, "we think he's doing well considering all he's been through. Probably he'll periodically go on binges of uncontrollable behavior, but with time, those binges should grow less frequent and less intense. So all we have to suggest is that you keep on as you have and see us in August to discuss proper first-grade placement. We can help you with the schools."

When we left the center that afternoon, we were a family—an independent unit. Oh, we would always depend on others, but we would decide when, where, and upon whom. We held no illusions of a smooth road ahead. Jake would continue to bedevil his sister, and he and Steven would occasionally clash. The school would frequently call us for conferences, and I would often wonder how he could exasperate me so.

But no matter, now he was our child, not the agency's. He was, in fact, so much ours, that we would begin sending contributions to the agency again.

There comes a time when a family has grown, with strength, into such a unit that the agency can no longer perform its task of mediator-interpreter. The parents know the child, and the child knows the parents. They have grown dependent upon each other, and with that dependency, they have moved away from the protective arm of the agency. The caseworker who visits monthly cannot predict the child's behavior, and no longer can she arbitrate disputes that clearly rise from the differences among the involved individuals. The family has assumed its own responsibilities.

Like the mother who recognizes the time when her infant is ready to move from breast to cup, the agency begins its withdrawal from the life of the family. Your particular circumstance will determine how and when this weaning begins; it can, in fact, be rather traumatic if it catches you unaware, but it is a vote of confidence, for it indicates that the agency realizes that you have progressed as a family to the point at which you have earned the right to succeed on your own.

After months of dependency on the agency, you may resemble the college freshman who wishes that his parents' confidence in him had not sent him so far from home. But, if you have been honest with your caseworker, the agency's withdrawal from the scene will provoke only passing anxiety. Problems will still need resolving, and discouragement will sometimes be present, but this, after all, is the way with any family—whether adopted or not. Family life has never been Utopia.

Legalities

State laws vary to such a degree that you should examine carefully the legalities of your own area. What is most important to your family is your awareness that a final order of adoption binds a child to you just as stringently as though he had been born to you. You are answerable to the law for his well-being, his behavior, and the rights of inheritance.

Legal adoption of an older child is often delayed beyond the fulfillment of state requirements until such time as the most difficult problems have become manageable. You cannot expect, however, to have achieved a euphoric existence before you file for permanent parenthood. No child reaches adulthood without causing his parents headaches, but you and your caseworker can determine at what point your family relationship has so stabilized itself that the adoption can proceed with a reasonable certainty of success.

You should not regard the agency as a disinterested party because it no longer holds legal responsibility. The intricate nature of the adoption of an older child produces a far-reaching relationship between you and the caseworker. The caseworker will have visited you more frequently than would have been the case had you adopted an infant. Even though yours may have been a fairly crisis-free adjustment, you will have talked in more depth with the caseworker, for the experience of adopting an older child will have given you more to discuss. The caseworker will know your child as an individual, not as a baby whose personality is only emerging. Thus, you and the agency will become interwoven. When the caseworker no longer schedules regular visits, your relationship becomes similar to that of neighbors who have moved to different towns. Your interest does not fade, and correspondence, perhaps limited to lengthy notes on Christmas cards, will testify to your continued interest. Like you and your personal friends, the caseworker moves on to establish other relationships, but if any difficulty surfaces, the agency is anxious to assist if you can use its help. Though no longer on the scene, the concern of the agency will not have vanished. You should feel free to ask for help, no matter how much time has elapsed.

You may feel disappointed that the long-awaited day when you receive the final adoption papers fails to kindle the anticipated elation. But how could it be otherwise? For adoption is gradual, and he became yours on a day-to-day basis as he and you took each tentative step toward each other. That decree-in-hand document is merely legal recognition of the family you have created.

11 Epilogue

After nine months, we had reconciled ourselves to his nighttime problems and allowed him to play quietly in his bed in semidarkness until he accepted sleep. Though kissed goodnight at 7:30, Jake usually lay awake until 8:30, the hour of Polly's bedtime. As long as he heard the television or our voices, he seemed content with the routine.

But one night, when we had company, he could not be appeased by this compromise. In and out of bed, he tormented Polly and interrupted our conversation. As the hours passed, our patience grew short. Conciliation failed, as did threats and a sound paddling. In desperation, I began one of those foolish lectures to which all parents are prone. Defiantly rigid, he lay there, weighing every word I uttered.

"I know you've had some hard knocks, but you're a pretty lucky boy," I said. "God made you healthy and that's lucky." Silence. "God made you pretty sharp and that's lucky, too," I continued. Silence. "And though you don't think so now, you're pretty lucky that God gave you to us to love and take care of."

Suddenly, he bolted upright in his bed and refuted, "God didn't give me to you. It was the Children's Home Society!"

I like to think that today's Jake would not think he must absolve God of the terrible act of placing him with us. I sometimes wonder if he would respond in the same way to the same lecture if I repeated it tonight, but I am not about to give him the opportunity.

People say that he has changed considerably in his years of being our child. His father and I cannot identify any marked changes, though occasionally we recall an incident that leads us to conclude he has moved a long way—but so has Polly in the same amount of time.

Unquestionably, he has turned our life topsy-turvy, and

Polly now understands why her friends thought her crazy to want a brother or a sister. Yet, like most siblings, she misses his taunts when he is sick or away for the night. Steven, a man in his mid-forties, finds Jake's never-ending energy a drain on his own, especially when he is approached in the driveway each evening with a "Let's play ball." Although Steven would prefer a cold beer as a means of unwinding, he often yields and half an hour later returns to the house refreshed from shooting basketball with his son. As for myself, I daily dread the inevitable bickering, the never-ending upheaval, and the clashes that stem from Jake's attempts to be a dictator in a household that adheres to the principle of parental authority. But when I see him walking down the driveway in his jaunty manner or feel the peck he spontaneously gives my cheek, I smile both inside and out, regardless of the trials of the day. Jake is a complication to this family as, of course, he should be.

I find myself tempted to write the expected cliché that we love him just as though he had been born to us, but I fight that impulse because, of course, he was not born to us. All four of us are realistic. We know that he is adopted and we do not pretend otherwise. However, the very circumstances of our being allowed to raise him make him special, just as Polly is special because she was born to us. Indeed, he *is* special, as is every individual, simply because of the uniqueness of himself.

When we brought him home, I would have doubted that a child in a loving, well-intentioned environment would carry insecurities for so many months. I was naive, perhaps stupid. The death of an infant more than a decade ago can still provoke intense feelings in Steven and me if we allow ourselves too much retrospection. Knowing that we bear scars from the past, how could we dare to assume that Jake's scars would disappear so quickly? We are told that children are resilient. Undoubtedly, they are. But *resilience* is not synonymous with *callousness*, and to expect the child to suddenly forget the old and take on the new requires a certain insensitivity. We thank God that Jake is not a callous person.

Scarred though he is by what his immature mind would label his abandonment, he has begun to love again. First he loved his sister; more slowly, he has grown to love us. Hearing him boast of an all "A" report card, a stranger would never guess that this brash youngster falls asleep midst stuffed animals that occasionally he forsakes in the early morning hours when, waking from bad dreams, he sneaks into bed with his parents. Nor, of course, would the stranger know that the report card ranked him disappointingly low—not in his academic subjects, but in behavior. You see, our child knows the harshness of the world. He recognized upon sight that the report card would provide his peers with a striking point. Since only his parents needed to see the card, he determined to forestall any teasing, so he lied. He wants no more jabs at what he feels are his weaknesses. As long as he needs to protect himself with this armor of invulnerability, we will grant him our cooperation—not by lying for him or by shielding him from the truth, but by not betraying his vulnerability to his friends. We have made him return stolen pennies, but we refuse to humiliate him by requiring an honest answer to a playmate's casual question, "How'd you do this time?" His self-worth is not yet securely enough established that he can admit any weakness to the world, but he has admitted his weaknesses to himself, to us, and to his sister (to whom he elected to tell the truth about his grades). We call that progress.

We are confident that he will eventually discard this face he has created for the world because his inherent strength will invalidate the need. In the meantime, we will sometimes agonize over him, throw up our hands in despair, but, mostly, we will enjoy this young boy who, for a few years, is lent to us by the Children's Home Society—and also God.